LIVERPOOL
city of architecture

Quentin Hughes

The Bluecoat Press

Contents

Foreword

When Liverpool was selected as one of the three finalists by the Arts Council of Great Britain for its 'City of Architecture and Design' award in 1994, the reaction nationally was predictable – 'Liverpool? Why Liverpool?'

The answer would have been self-evident had the latest publication by Quentin Hughes been available at the time. Containing, as it does, not only a pictorial architectural gazetteer of Liverpool's architectural splendour, both ancient and modern, but also an exemplary synopsis of the city's architectural evolution, *Liverpool: City of Architecture* demonstrates eloquently why this great city could lay claim to the coveted title with justifiable confidence and pride.

In the event, Liverpool won for England since the other two finalists were both Scottish cities. As the reader of this book will readily conclude from the evidence it contains, Liverpool richly deserved its place in the finals both for its architectural inheritance and its vigorous development of new design that will become, we hope, the proud inheritance of future generations of Liverpudlians. As Professor Hughes concludes, there is in Liverpool 'a splendid panorama from many generations which is a rich heritage well worth caring for and, indeed, boasting about'. I trust that you, the reader, will agree and be proud to boast about this great 'city of architecture'.

Peter Toyne DL, BA (Hon), DEd, CIMgt, FRSA
Vice-Chancellor of the Liverpool John Moores University

Introduction

I seem to be getting into the habit of writing gazetteers, Malta, one on Gibraltar and now this one which is really an up-date of the little book I wrote for Studio Vista in 1968. There would seem to be two ways in which to describe the architectural splendours of Liverpool, and I have tried to incorporate them both in this book. The first part is an essay that sketches in the development of the most important characteristics of both the architecture and the building engineering in the city and describes some of the work done over the ages by its notable designers. This is to provide a panorama of the place. The second part is a gazetteer in chronological order that traces the development to maturity and beyond of those buildings that remain, and of a few important ones that have been destroyed, of the growth of one of the great ports of the world. The meteoric expansion depicted in the growing richness and increased individuality of its buildings became part of the fabric of what was once the richest provincial city in the world. A city, too, with civic pride which it could promote and extol in its great municipal buildings which vie in splendour and monumentality with any elsewhere. And, because the place is comparatively small, the concentration of architecture is more spellbinding.

I suppose I am a puritan at heart. I do not like musical composers making jokes, nor do I like architectural designers playing games. I may get a small intellectual satisfaction deciphering Mannerist tendencies, but the products pall after a while – an architectural joke soon becomes a stale joke. The trouble really is that we have become so eclectic in our taste, surrounded by such a plethora of styles that we are inclined to accept anything and reject nothing, and this leads a critic into inconsistency. In the book the reader will find comments that are contradictory but, at least, I have tried to make comment and not just to confine my remarks to a description of the historical facts. Perhaps I have followed Pevsner, but with less gusto and self-assurance. This attitude may soon make my contribution dated so you are advised to buy the book now and read it soon, always being able to enjoy the wealth of colour photography.

Writing a gazetteer is often a hazardous undertaking, especially when one is incorporating older material. Not that the buildings change all that much, nor that the comments on their architecture are no longer valid, but these days their uses change rapidly; what starts out to be a bank is suddenly transformed into a solicitor's office, what was once a church becomes a secondhand furniture warehouse, and what was designed as a fine civic building may be left an empty shell seeking a suitable use. Change is inevitable and not necessarily a bad thing, but the recent rate of change in Liverpool can be decidedly disturbing.

Sometimes the conversions are successful. but often the old buildings remain as aesthetic shells screening interiors to which they have little relevance.

Liverpool: City of Architecture has taken many years to prepare and, during those years, I have received help and encouragement from many people; too many, in fact, for all to receive individual mention, but I would like to single out some of those who have been most helpful, in particular, Colin Wilkinson for researching and organising the photography and bringing the project to fruition, Michael March for the design and layout of the book, Angela Mounsey who scanned in most of the photographs and Barbara Brodie and Margaret Hirst who typed much of the original manuscript. The late Edward Hubbard read the original proofs and gave me valuable advice which, from his vast store of knowledge, he readily dispensed. John Vaughan has kindly laboured through this text and offered many suggestions which I have included in my revision. Tim Olden kindly gave me the information about Carl Bartels. But my particular thanks go to Maggi Morris who has walked with me, commenting on many of the buildings we have seen and who has given me her valuable research notes on the intricacies of some. I acknowledge her help most gratefully.

Finding the way

The layout of Liverpool is fairly simple. To the west lie the broad waters of the Mersey, bordered by a long line of docks, now largely abandoned by commercial shipping and in the process of being converted to other purposes. At the pivot stands the Pier Head group of buildings, architectural symbols of the city. Then a grid-shaped wedge, the old core of the town, runs east. Where the ground starts to rise stands the plateau and there they built the main civic buildings of the city, St George's Hall, the Art Gallery and the Museum, and from thence roads radiate like the spokes of a half-wheel, its rim the peripheral artery of Queen's Drive. About half way along these spokes the ground rises again to a semi-circular crest upon which were built the noble terrace houses of the Georgian style. Up to the 1930s this was more or less the limit of the city; now the radials fly further out, embracing older villages and large areas of suburban growth richly interspersed, especially to the south, with parkland. Beyond, is a succession of new towns and communities built to relieve the pressure on the central area and rehouse those who had been forced to live in slums – Knotty Ash, Clubmoor, Huyton, Childwall Valley and Speke.

This is a simplification of the pattern, but it serves to give a general picture of a scene into which fit the buildings described and illustrated in this book.

Because Liverpool expanded as a great seaport in the second half of the 19th century, many of its finest buildings are the offices built for the shipping and insurance companies which formed their headquarters there, and these are to be found in the core, the area defined by the parliamentary division called Exchange. There too rose the major civic buildings, built to run the municipal administration of the city and display with pride its civic splendour.

Where the ground rises to the crest of hills stand the two great cathedrals, facing each other along the length of Hope Street and near there were built the main buildings of the two universities whose expansions gave, and are giving, much of the impetus to modern architecture in the 1960s and today.

In order to help readers track down the various buildings, each one has an address followed by a number that indicates the postal area of Liverpool in which it can be found. Readers who are strangers to Liverpool are also referred to *Liverpool A-Z*, published by the Geographers' A-Z Map Company, Sevenoaks, and particularly to the coloured edition which is so much easier to read, where the exact location of every street is marked.

People and places

This is an attempt to show through the existing buildings of Liverpool, and by means of some that have not been so lucky as to survive, the development from humble origins into what was to become the finest city of architecture in the country. To tell this story I have been selective for there is so much rich material to describe and my preferences show through. The city is constantly undergoing change and buildings designed for one era are adapted for a new one. This often changes their character, particularly when the setting in which they stand is changed. The scale of the city fluctuated from modest origins to a monumental grandeur at the beginning of this century, only to start to be reduced by the sweeping away of most of those vast structures, the warehouses, which once dominated the Dock Road, and was further diminished by the gaps which inevitably have appeared in the street fabric. Those open spaces which were left have not, in most cases, been reshaped as civic entities – as spaces which mean something in architectural terms. But one must praise the policy of planting trees on open sites no longer required for development.

In this edition I have included some of the sculpture of Liverpool which was often as architectural in expression as the buildings that stood in its vicinity.

Much of the written material was presented originally in *Liverpool*, that little guide book published by Studio Vista in 1969, and long since out of print. In fact, it was an instant sellout, never reprinted until now. In this book all the photographs are new and most are now in colour and the text revised and augmented.

And so to the background of Liverpool town. Way back in history they began to build a castle on the banks of the River Mersey. It was begun by William de Ferrers about 1235 and was quite strong for it consisted of four round corner towers embracing a square courtyard. Its most interesting feature, and this was novel, was the way in which the curtain wall that faced onto the river was canted in two directions so that archers could throw flanking fire across this splayed front from the adjoining towers onto an attacker from the sea. Now nothing remains of the castle and on its site stands the statue of Queen Victoria [160]. But, at the time of the Civil War it was still intact, although in a poor state, when the royalist engineer, Bernard de Gomme, proposed, in 1644, to form it into a citadel surrounded by a bastion trace to hold Liverpool against the Roundheads. From its walls a strong line of bastions would have swung in an arc to encircle the little town and secure the haven. However, the fortifications were not built; only some earthworks by the Parliamentarians. As the town grew, buildings hemmed in the castle and Castle Street was laid out from the Town Hall to the new dock. Eventually on that site the Customs House [38] was built.

Liverpool grew to greatness in the 19th century when her port thrived, carrying to the New World the manufactured goods of Lancashire and the Midlands. The flavour of the city is therefore Victorian and Edwardian with a tinge of magnificence carried to the outbreak of the First World War. In the central area, surrounded by later structures, the Bluecoat Buildings [8] stand out as an isolated gem of an earlier age. John Wood's Town Hall [9], the only other early building, was reclothed and domed in the 19th century so that its appearance is now in keeping with its adjoining offices in Castle Street.

Inspired by the heroism of the Greek War of Independence in the early years of the 19th century and with an eye to emulating the beauty of Ancient Greece as a reminder that free democratic development can go hand in hand with architectural beauty, Liverpool architects threw themselves into the task of creating a modern northern Athens. Buildings modelled on ancient Greek temples began to appear throughout the city. This

An artist's impression of how Liverpool Castle might have looked.

move was not unique to Liverpool: it is found elsewhere in the country at that time and particularly in the North West. But two architects who worked in Liverpool stand out. John Foster Junior (c1786-1846) was the second son of John Foster, the Surveyor to the Corporation. In 1810, the young Foster went on the Grand Tour. From all accounts he was rather indolent with an eye for the ladies but, in Istanbul, then Constantinople, he met Charles Robert Cockerell (1788-1863), another young architect who was to enthuse him with a love of Greek architecture and release a fund of pent up energy. The two became lifelong friends. In the spring of the following year they were to discover the famous Ægina marbles and, soon after that, the architectural reliefs in Arcadia known as the Phigaleian marbles, now in the British Museum. These were archaeological and architectural finds of the first order and they set young Foster on the path of studying and copying Greek architecture, a style in which he soon became an expert. On his return to Liverpool, he cast himself enthusiastically into practice, the results of which can be seen in this book. In particular, I must mention here his little Greek temple [37], modelled on ancient precedent and a charming example of the style. It is sad that so many of his fine Grecian buildings have been destroyed. Some, like the facade of St Catherine's Church, could have been saved. Although the church was bombed in the blitz, its stone Ionic portico stood intact at one end of Abercromby Square [34] and could have been incorporated into the facade of the new University Senate House [218].

Cockerell also came to work in Liverpool where he designed the Branch Bank of England [69] and completed St George's Hall [56] after the death of Elmes, being largely responsible for the design of the small concert hall with its Greek caryatids supporting the balconies. Foster and Cockerell were an interesting pair of architects

for, not only were they steeped in ancient Greek culture, they both were interested in the problems of modern architecture, Foster being responsible for the design of the impressive iron structure of St John's Market [30] and Cockerell working on the problem of lighting the interiors of office buildings in a gloomy northern climate.

The Greek movement reached its climax with the building of young Harvey Lonsdale Elmes' design for St George's Hall. Admittedly the general shape of that great hall was Roman – it had to be, for the Greeks had never had the means to construct so large an enclosed space – but the detail is pure and exquisite Greek.

The Greek Revival saw a late flowering in Liverpool. It was partly due to the enthusiasm of men like Professor Sir Charles Reilly (1874-1948) and partly to the close connection with America where there was a similar revival. Merchants passed to and fro between Liverpool and New York and with them went all sorts of ideas; the link was close. Reilly's Students Union Building for the University [172], the extension to the College of Art [131], the Empire Theatre and the Bank of West Africa in Water Street [179] are good examples in which all the details are pure Greek. Reilly, who was head of the influential University School of Architecture, set his students the task of making measured drawings of classical buildings and was instrumental in building up a close relationship with American architects, encouraging Liverpool students to work in their offices during the vacations. It was even proposed to erect a giant Greek Doric column in the courtyard of the School building.

Liverpool's architectural growth was part of a world of commerce. 'In Liverpool decent chaps owned ships, fairly decent chaps broked cotton, almost decent chaps broked corn – the rest just didn't exist'. This was the impression of a visitor, heightened by the monumental quality of the city offices and the impressive solidity of Jesse

Hartley's dockland. With Liverpool, it was the scale which first impressed – a scale quite different from other English cities – she built high, reminiscent of her American sisters, linked across the North Atlantic trade route. She built wide and expansively when laying out her civic centre – a pattern not seen south of Edinburgh.

But it was the docks that made all this possible and Liverpool was indeed fortunate in its choice of dock engineer. Jesse Hartley (1780-1860) was a Yorkshireman, blunt and forthright, but he was also a first-rate civil engineer. He had four other qualities: foresight, imagination, aesthetic taste and persistence. He was appointed in 1824 and ruled there for 36 years. By using every trick in the book and a brute determination he would push forward his ideas to completion and it was on the fruition of these ideas that the great Port of Liverpool was built. Not only could he plan on a bold scale, but he paid meticulous attention to the smallest point so that the details of his masonry are a pleasure to observe. He was also a romantic who believed strongly in the use of architectural symbolism. Why else but to suggest the strength and security of his dockland would he have designed his buildings to resemble medieval castles? His Victoria Tower [68], put there to tell the time, and his several pump houses whose function was to raise energy for the dock gates and the cranes, are all fitted with machicolation, drop boxes and imitation arrow slits. Even the gates he built for admittance to the docks are designed so that their thick wooden panels slide into prepared slots to seal so that scarcely a rat could enter. Nancy Ritchie-Noakes *Jesse Hartley: Dock Engineer to the Port of Liverpool 1824-60* is an indispensable guide to any visit to the docks.

The buildings which form the Pier Head group have become so familiar to us that we no longer question their form, and yet a careful analysis would reveal interesting points. The Royal Liver Building [170], designed by W Aubrey Thomas (1908), a much neglected architect of considerable ability, is the most powerful of the group. Thomas' originality can be discerned in the State Fire Assurance Office in Dale Street (1906) [164] where he is seen to be developing through a phase of late Gothic with the easy flowing lines of Art Nouveau. It makes an unusual office block and Thomas had considerable difficulty in the design as he had to persuade two disassociated clients to come together in order to provide the land for his comprehensive design utilising two gabled bays flanking an oriel tower. Aubrey Thomas' next important commission, begun in the same year, was Tower Building [166] which flanks the Dock Road, clad throughout in white glazed tile to shed the film of dirt deposited by the city's atmosphere. It must be one of the earliest steel-framed buildings in this country – Mewes & Davies used this method of construction on the Ritz Hotel in London two years earlier. No precise style was adopted when building Tower Building. These herald the century when, with a conscious effort, architects broke away from the decorative influences of the past. The windows are large, allowing abundant light to flood the building. The central tower forecasts his later work in the Royal Liver Building, and is similar to that truncated form of the Liver towers which may be seen in early photographs during the course of their construction. But the Royal Liver Friendly Society Building [170] is his chef-d'oeuvre. This massive 20th century structure has no counterpart in England and is one of the world's earliest essays in multi-storey reinforced concrete construction – not that one could tell this from the exterior. Its side elevations remind one of HH Richardson's work in Chicago. Its bulk towers across the waterfront and is the most characteristic image of Liverpool. A grey stone, darkened with age, supports two sculptural domed clock towers surmounted by those mythical Liver birds. The modelling of the towers is derived from Art Nouveau, yet the handling of the pieces is very individual. The foundation stone was laid in 1908 and the building finished in 1911.

The offices of the Mersey Docks and Harbour Board [169], designed by Arnold Thornley in collaboration with Briggs and Wolstenholme, came earlier and work began in 1907. What pomp and magnificence prompted the design of the headquarter building! Commonplace in an age of office structures, we no longer feel surprised at the idea of placing the dome of St Paul's on the centre of a Renaissance palace. But, of course, the dome is not that of St Paul's – it is, in fact, taken almost piecemeal from a design made by Professor Reilly for the Anglican Cathedral competition of 1902.

Last of the waterfront buildings is the Cunard [176], designed by Willink and Thicknesse in 1914 and constructed during the war. This gap filler is another mighty essay in the power of this century's commercial enterprises. It is like an Italian palazzo draped in Greek detail: a 20th century revival almost unique to Liverpool in this country. As previously noted, it echoes developments in America, and the style can be seen in numerous buildings. The Cunard Building is clad in Portland stone, heavily tooled, with a strong rusticated base and a powerfully-carved cornice. Its chiaroscuric effect is created not by light but by the wind-swept rain which carries soot into the crevices and down the lines of the side elevations, leaving exposed protrusions a gleaming white. Here is a lesson in building in our north-western climatic setting which has not gone unheeded. Brian Westwood, before he designed his University Mathematics Building [199], paid special attention to the detailing of the Cunard Building.

Until recently, the long red thread of Europe's first overhead railway [142] drew a latticed line across the backs of these buildings and the fine adjoining tower of Herbert Rowse's Mersey Tunnel Ventilating Shaft [192]. The railway has now gone, leaving an impressive motor road of dimensions quite unusual in our cities. But this width is by no means unusual in Liverpool. Thanks to a considered early policy by John Alexander Brodie (1858-1934), the City Engineer, many of the tram lines in the suburban fringes were run on central grazed strips; and when the trams were scrapped, these were cleared and trees planted so that the city inherited wide fringes of arterial boulevards bordered by ample double track roadways. Let us hope that the proposed new tram or rapid transport system does not destroy these fine forest trees.

Liverpool has always been remarkable for its far-sightedness, not least in the courage of its patronage. Both St George's Hall [56] (Harvey Lonsdale Elmes, 1838, completed by CR Cockerell), probably the finest Neo-Classical structure in Europe, and the great Anglican Liverpool Cathedral [161] (Sir Giles Gilbert Scott. 1902, assisted in its early stages by Bodley), now completed on St James' Mount, a building whose true qualities are only now becoming apparent, were designed by architects in their early twenties. Nor should one forget the importance of the appointment of Jesse Hartley to develop the dockland and, more recently, Graeme Shankland to prepare dynamic proposals for the refurbishing of the city centre.

In the context of the Anglican Cathedral it could be said that Liverpool saw the birth and death of the Gothic Revival. When the Gothic style was first introduced on a large scale, as for instance in Horace Walpole's Strawberry Hill, it was no more than a plaything, and so through the 18th century this attitude persisted. One man changed all this. Thomas Rickman (1776-1841) was not a particularly gifted architect, but he must be praised for his industry and for the way he directed the Gothic Revival. He started work in a chemist's shop and later on became an accountant in Liverpool, but he was drawn to architecture. His work was meticulous and showed almost Germanic thoroughness. He sketched thousands of Gothic details and toured, studying the mediaeval churches of the North West.

Only the sort of mind which could, as a hobby, direct the fabrication of an army of hand-painted toy soldiers could entertain so thorough an investigation, such as characterises Rickman's work. Although we may find him most interesting for having produced three cast iron churches in Liverpool, his major importance attaches to his unravelling of the pattern of mediaeval Gothic architecture. It was Rickman who coined the now famous terms, Early English, Decorated and Perpendicular, and it was he who in his *Attempt to discriminate the styles of architecture in England, from the Conquest to the Reformation* (London, 1817), set Gothic Revival on its path of erudition which crystallised in the crusade of Pugin and Ruskin. If this book was the birth of Gothic Revival, the Anglican Cathedral tolls its death knell. When the competition was launched in 1900 the Cathedral Committee stipulated that the design should be in 'the Gothic style'. This announcement brought forth a howl of protest in the national press, for, although few English architects had as yet formulated their ideas on a new style, most of these with serious intentions and avant-garde predilections discarded a dependence on the past. Heard at that time were phrases like 'architecture should be something living and not a dead imitation of past work' and suggestions 'in favour of all our art being expressive of the great movement of the thought and aspirations of today in a living language'. Nevertheless, Gilbert Scott's winning design was Gothic – a final blaze of Gothic on an unprecedented scale – a fitting consummation of a great period.

Perhaps it is being greedy, but how splendid would have been the civic centre had both the Assize Courts and St George's Hall been built as separate buildings and John Foster Junior's classical facade for Lime Street Station (1835) retained. All are illustrated in the drawing which formed the frontispiece to Dr Boswell Reid's *Illustrations of the Theory and Practice of Ventilation* (London, 1844). Reid was the remarkable engineer called in by Harvey Lonsdale Elmes to ventilate his great buildings. But then we would have lost the opportunity of having the Walker Art Gallery [120] and the County Sessions House [130] which, had the separate Assize Courts been built, would have been obscured, and also Alfred Waterhouse's North Western Hotel [118]. Even the great arches over the train sheds at Lime Street Station [108] might never have been built.

There is another side to the development of architecture. Without technical innovations the building of the many new and large structures of the 19th century would not have been possible. Only a revolution in building construction could make them feasible. From the latter part of the 18th century a series of innovations and inventions reshaped architecture. The amazing thing is that most of them either saw their birth in Liverpool or were found there early in their development. This can be partly explained by the fact that the stupendous commercial expansion of the city attracted entrepreneurs who were prepared to experiment in a climate less oppressive than that found in the capital.

Within the field of architectural construction, which is the backbone of fine building, one can see five major developments: the use of iron to hold up a building, the ability to make buildings fireproof; the idea of providing a thin cladding, not part of the structural frame but just to keep out the weather; the use of large steel and concrete frames which permitted the construction of multi-storey buildings and, finally, the idea of making buildings out of large prefabricated panels.

The first innovation, where iron is used to support the structure, began with the idea of supporting the encircling galleries of churches on thin iron columns so as to cause the minimum obstruction to the view of the preacher. The earliest example was probably St Anne's Church in Liverpool, built in 1772 but now demolished. This was followed by St James [10] built two years later. From these humble beginnings sprang the great iron structures of the 19th century. The craze to display cast iron from larger and larger castings, reached its zenith in Liverpool. The whole of the frontispiece, that classical Tuscan portico, of the Dock Traffic Office at the Albert Dock [71] was cast and fabricated in iron. Where else can one find such a display of technical dexterity in iron?

The idea of using iron to construct a building was carried further in Rickman's iron churches [24 & 26] where he devised a system, assisted by John Cragg's ideas, that was prefabricated in cast iron and could thus be mass produced, was fireproof, was quick to erect and which was dry on erection. Unlike brick and stone buildings which

Eldon Street flats, a pioneeing exercise in the use of reinforced panels, shortly before demolition.

took about a year to dry out, Rickman's churches could, after a coat of paint, be used the next day.

Fireproof construction was developed in the factories of the North West and in the great warehouses of Liverpool. The Albert Dock Warehouses (1839-45) [55] are a fine example being built entirely of stone, brick and iron. Supported on cast iron columns spanned by wrought iron beams and roofed with metal plates, there was no inflammable timber in the whole building.

The idea of cladding a building with a thin waterproof membrane, in this case largely glass, seems to have been thought out by Peter Ellis (1804-1884) and first used on his office building, Oriel Chambers [101], in 1864. The facade of the courtyard is cantilevered nearly a metre out from its iron frame and is clad with thin panels of glass and stone. As a result, this becomes one of the first great examples of modern architecture; the germ that developed into the glass-clad office buildings of our time. The courtyard of Ellis' second office building, 16 Cook Street [102], is similar but with the addition of a metal and glass-clad iron spiral staircase.

To stack floor upon floor and achieve the skyscrapers needed to house the offices of commerce it was necessary to devise a frame of steel or reinforced concrete. This the Americans began to do in New York and Chicago. Probably the earliest example of the large steel frame in England is the Ritz Hotel in London, followed by the White Star Offices [146] and the Royal Insurance Company Building [147] in Liverpool. The first really large reinforced concrete office building in the world was the Royal Liver Building [170] built by Aubrey Thomas at the Pier Head in Liverpool.

Finally, the idea of omitting a frame and depending for support on a series of reinforced concrete panels was to emerge from the fertile brain of Alexander Brodie (1858-1934), 'a giant among engineers'. From 1898 to 1925 he was City Engineer to Liverpool and it was then that he invented and built such a system on the flats at Eldon Street. He used it also on the tram stables at Walton [167]. The idea did not really take on in England although there is a report of a prefabricated house consisting of 15 large concrete panels, which included walls, floors, ceilings and a staircase, being ordered by someone in Letchworth in 1909 as a result of Brodie's entry in the Cheap Cottages Exhibition. The house was built in three days and cost £200 of which £50 went on transporting the panels from Liverpool. The system, largely neglected in

13

The splendour of the Royal Liver Building reflected the economic importance of Liverpool in the early years of the 20th century.

Britain, was taken up all over the world, particularly in the countries of Eastern Europe. It is ironical that, when Liverpool Corporation wanted to erect tall flats in Sheil Park, they had to commission a French company to provide the Camus system which was based on Brodie's original invention.

The story of Liverpool, like that of all great cities, is full of 'might have beens' and interesting though it may be to speculate on the effect they might have had, one must also remember that a city is in a continuous state of change and good can follow good given the right circumstances, the money and the architectural inspiration. Had the city planners had their way the Royal Liver Building [170] would have looked just like the Mersey Docks and Harbour Board Building [169]. One is fine but two would have been unutterably boring, so we must be thankful that Aubrey Thomas was permitted to realise his eccentric masterpiece. The great opportunity that was missed was the building of Sir Edwin Lutyens's vast Metropolitan Cathedral, a building of immense proportions, that would have outclassed everything in the city and have been the largest cathedral in the world. It was also a splendid design with powerful bulky walls, reminiscent of Michelangelo, forming the platform for an immense dome. Alas, only the crypt was completed for, in 1939, the war came and the two driving forces, Archbishop Downey and Sir Edwin Lutyens, both died. Money ran short and attitudes changed in the hopeful years that followed the ending of the Second World War when social reconstruction took precedent over monument building. Perhaps it was already an anachronism and one must realise that, had it been built, it would have dominated the urban setting, dwarfed all the surrounding buildings and made a nonsense of Alfred Waterhouse's University Victoria Buildings [136] which would have wilted in the shade. But it would have been magnificent!

In many architectural fields the years between the two great wars were years of stagnation. The modern movement hardly touched the city's buildings. Ruben's store, later the Co-operative Society's store in London Road but now empty, with its Mendelssonian expression, most nearly approached the avant-garde work of Western Europe. The Majestic Cinema, also in London Road but now demolished, bent the ideas of the European School to that strange modernistic flavour of a cinematic world. The other inter-war cinemas, like the Carlton, Tuebrook and the Abbey at Wavertree, were watered down versions of Cinema Modernistic. The achievements in Corporation housing were impressive, but the style, though attractive, was conservative and Neo-Georgian. Herbert J Rowse (1887-1963) was the most powerful architectural figure in inter-war Liverpool. His large structures and ambitious projects – Martins Bank [183], the India Building [180] and the Mersey Tunnel [181] – are in his own brand of classical design, produced not without a knowledge of the work of others in modern architecture. Only in the Philharmonic Hall [190] does he marshal this knowledge to produce a building strongly tinged by the Dutch influence of Dudok.

The post-war period was one of new growth, slow at first, making good some of the extensive war damage, but gathering momentum in the 1960s. Liverpool was slow to recover and therefore avoided the errors inflicted on some other bomb-damaged English cities. As a result, many fine old buildings which might otherwise have been demolished were preserved for a period when they would be appreciated again. Slum clearance and rehousing have been, and remain, problems of immense proportions and much money and thought has been expended on trying to solve those problems. Although mistakes have been made, Liverpool has a better record than any other city in attempting to provide decent housing for the poor and needy.

Liverpool has been fortunate in its public servants. Three stand out in this story. Lyster, Brodie and Keay.

George Fosbery Lyster (1821-1899) was largely responsible for the enlargement of the docks between 1861 and 1890, having succeeded Jesse Hartley's son as engineer-in-chief to the Mersey Docks and Harbour Board. Spending about £20 million, he increased the quayside accommodation for shipping from 20 to 34 miles – a vast undertaking. One of his interesting ideas, which probably would not have worked, was to moor floating batteries at the mouth of the Mersey, armed with gigantic 110-ton muzzle loading guns as a deterrent against the threat of German raiders. Lyster taught Brodie. Alexander Brodie (1858-1934) was a man of infinite resource. His exploits with concrete panels have been described above. He is also credited with the invention of the football goal net. One would think it an easy matter to design a football goal, but no, it required the application of engineering logic to design a net into which the ball always penetrated and would in no way bounce out. But more important in the context of this study was his layout of roads. He became the Haussmann of Liverpool, inventing and planning the idea of running trams in central green reservations between double carriageways so that Liverpool, in the 1930s, led the country in the provision of wide avenues, now planted with forest trees, which radiate out from the city centre to join Brodie's fine ring road, Queen's Drive. This tree-lined avenue swung in a great arc around the city from Sefton Park in the south to Walton in the North. Another ring further out, King's Drive, was planned but never built until the construction of the orbital motorway. On the edges of Queen's Drive and in clusters beyond, the City Architect, Sir Lancelot Keay (1883-1974) laid out mile on mile of Neo-Georgian housing estates [188]. Terrace houses of considerable elegance and charm, many with open gardens in the American manner, provided a new standard of living for those families moved out from the crowded city slums. Each cluster had its shopping centre, the shops being faced with elegant columnar porticoes to protect shoppers from the rain and sun. It was a very civilised solution the quality of which has not been fully appreciated. Dare one say it was too good for some to appreciate for vandalism has taken its toll, and privatisation along with weak planning control has permitted many purchasers to assert their own poor taste and wreck the unity of this fine design. Architectural anarchy may have its charm but not when perpetrated on Neo-Georgian terraces. As if that were not enough, by ill luck, many of the trees that had been planted on the verges and which had grown to maturity, were elm. They were struck down by the devastating Dutch Elm disease which rampaged across Britain.

Sir Lancelot Keay also created the new town of Speke which, at the time, was unique in municipal development. He was City Architect and Director of Housing in Liverpool from 1925 until 1948, responsible for building more than 35,000 houses and flats.

Keay was assisted by John Hughes (1903-1977), brilliant student of the Liverpool School of Architecture who carried off most of the design and construction prizes and was a finalist for the coveted Rome Scholarship. Hughes graduated with honours in 1931 and joined the staff of the City Architect. Then he was engaged in designing the large number of flats intended to provide convenient concentrated accommodation for workers in the docks and the city. On such a scale, they were unique outside London and the style was influenced by Piet Kramer and Michael de Klerk in Amsterdam and Josef Frank in Vienna. Already the features could be seen in Hughes' thesis design for a sports stadium, with its sweeping curves and long lines of streaked balcony passages. When a revulsion to multi-storey flats swept Britain in the 1980s, some of Hughes' buildings were demolished or allowed to fall into decay, but some have been modified and brought up to date only to destroy the rhythm and proportions of the original designs. Flat roofs may no longer be popular, but it is difficult to add a pitched roof to an existing building – the result is usually ugly.

Here it might be appropriate to mention the origins of the Liverpool School of Architecture for its influence on British architecture has been powerful. It was the first British university school to be established when Oxford and Cambridge, unlike the older European universities, clung to the idea that architecture was a subject unfit for university tuition. A hundred years ago, in 1883, the University of Liverpool appointed the first Roscoe Professor of Art, named after William Roscoe (1753-1831) that benefactor of the arts in the city. In the following year, an architect and architectural historian, Fred Simpson (1856-1928) was appointed to the chair. He and Sir Thomas Graham Jackson (1835-1924) devised a novel creation, the establishment of a school that would provide university education under one roof for all those engaged in the building process. Thus, architects were to be trained alongside painters, sculptors, builders, masons and carpenters. It would produce a school that locked together aesthetics, design and craftsmanship. This was a brilliant social experiment but, unfortunately, snobbery and prejudice eroded its execution. Few builders and craftsmen could be persuaded to join the course. Then came the Education Act of 1902 which hived off painting and sculpture to another institution run by the Corporation and they were formed into the City College of Art. Finally, Charles Reilly (1874-1949), at the age of 30, was appointed to the Roscoe Chair and, with tremendous gusto and enthusiasm, he converted the place from a 'school of architecture' to a 'school for architects'. His dynamic personality and bombast were to ensure that the School became well known across the world.

It is now possible to get the post-war period into some sort of historical perspective. It was a time when architects were experimenting with new materials and new methods of construction. It was also a time of feverish activity as the economy began to revive and the demand for a large number of new buildings became apparent. Because of the demand, architects made great effort to reduce the price of their products and, at the same time, increase output. The building trade and an inexperienced profession were not ready for the brave challenge. New materials were being produced but many had not been fully tested. The junction between one new product and another had, on occasion, been ill-considered and many of the builders lacked the experience of handling these new products. No wonder things went wrong – too much was asked for too quickly and too cheaply. Nevertheless, there were some notable successes and some were in Liverpool. To design its new buildings, the University commissioned national leaders who sometimes did not come up to expectations. But some of the fine results are illustrated in this book. Yorke, Rosenberg and Mardall's Electrical Engineering Building [205] was a bold, uncompromising statement and Gerald Beech's Wyncote Sports Pavilion [201] was one of the best examples of the modern style in the 1960s.

A renaissance of the city was reflected in the appointment of Graeme Shankland as planning consultant with instructions to provide a framework within the central area that could be redeveloped and largely rebuilt. His plan envisaged a 50mph motorway encircling the central area and using multi-level flyover junctions to lead traffic into car parks capable of holding 36,000 vehicles. Many of the shops were to face pedestrian precincts which were to be linked to form a continuous pedestrian way, unmatched in scale at the time by anything outside Venice. The proposals were developed and published in the form of reports which were issued approximately every two months. This was a welcome change from the traditional method of issuing one comprehensive report at the end of the design stage, as it provided topics for discussion and allowed some reappraisal during the design process. Sensitive to the heritage of the city, he commissioned the first British policy document on the conservation of urban areas.

This was a bold venture but, as has so often happened with town planning projects, it was no sooner submitted than the climate changed and the ideas became unpopular. It will probably take the passing of this generation before its contribution is fully appreciated.

In the 1960s the University of Liverpool blazed the trail of modern architecture, adopting the interesting policy of employing a number of well-known national architects to build a large precinct. Its policy was different from that adopted by many of the new

Lutyens' design for the Liverpool Metropolitan Cathedral, perhaps Liverpool's most significant architectual loss.

universities who tended to employ individual firms of architects to carry out their whole development programmes in a unified form. Liverpool chose variety of design, not always successful, but often lively and stimulating, creating interesting juxtapositions of many different shapes. This may one day be viewed as a bold venture in architectural patronage. Its main rebuilding programme complete by the 1980s, the University has, more recently, only required small additions, mainly conversions to the interiors of existing buildings such as the Liverpool School of Architecture and Building Engineering [221], the Students' Union [202] and the new Computer Centre housed in a converted non-conformist chapel. It might be said that the mantle has now fallen on the shoulders of the new Liverpool John Moores University which, with its buildings spread across the city, is now undertaking a large-scale programme of development and refurbishment. Under the leadership of a vice-chancellor keen on modern architecture and enthusiastic about the visual image of his city, fine new buildings and interesting conversions have started to appear. In particular, one must praise the new library, the Aldham Robart's Learning Resource Centre [226], probably the best recent building.

Liverpool is full of fine buildings. A gazetteer of this scale has to be selective. Half the fun of reading a gazetteer is to prove it wrong or inadequate and there is plenty of scope for that. The line had to be drawn somewhere and many good buildings have been left out, particularly some 19th century offices in the town centre. After all, one must remember that, excluding London, Liverpool has the largest number of listed buildings of any large city in the country. They could not all be illustrated. Fortunately my task has been made easier, for many of the later buildings, Corporation housing estates, blocks of flats and schools, have been well described and illustrated in *Liverpool Builds 1945-65* (Liverpool 1967) so that there has been no need to repeat much of the material described in that book. Others have been beautifully illustrated by David Wrightson in my book, *Seaport.*

The limit has been drawn at the city boundary, but there is much of interest beyond – large town centre redevelopment at Bootle, new towns at Skelmersdale and Runcorn, a school in Wallasey warmed by solar heat, the Port Sunlight village on the Wirral, Birkenhead's impressive Hamilton Square, the giant Ford factory at Halewood and the Squibb pharmaceutical factory across the Mersey, an example of Anglo-American collaboration in the design work. These are all developments which impinge on the character of Liverpool and some are in too close a perspective for us to focus accurately on their true values.

However, some actions have been so strong that their influence upon the architecture of the city cannot be denied. The most dramatic turn of events centered

An artist's impression of how Lutyens' Cathedral would have dominated the Liverpool skyline had it been completed.

around the riots in 1981 when part of Upper Parliament Street went up in flames. As a result the Government took action to revitalise the city and Michael Heseltine was made minister for Merseyside. Money was poured in and the Merseyside Development Corporation set up. It was decided to do something to the remains of the South Docks which were no longer used by shipping but which contained fine industrial buildings. The Albert Dock Warehouses [55] had long been fought over and there were threats to demolish them and fill in the dock for car parking, strongly opposed by the Merseyside Civic Society and the Victorian Society. Various proposals were made over the years to convert them into offices or into the Liverpool Polytechnic (now the Liverpool John Moores University) but all came to nothing as funds ran out. Then the Development Corporation was able to step in and restore this vast collection of buildings, the largest Grade 1 group in the country. It was a wonderful job, carried out with love and vigour, part being converted by James Stirling into the Tate Gallery of Liverpool [220], part into the Maritime Museum and the remainder into shops, restaurants, pubs, flats and offices. This has changed the picture of Liverpool turning it into a tourist attraction on a scale hitherto unimaginable to most of its citizens.

Although it takes more than money to produce good architecture, architecture is expensive. Liverpool, which grew to be one of the great ports of the world, whose name was carried on the stern of many of the large ships and liners, acquired riches almost beyond that of any other provincial 19th century city. But Liverpool changed in character as the nature of sea ports altered. By the 1960s, not only had much of the trade moved from the North West to the South East, but the nature of docking was changed fundamentally by the introduction of large tankers and container ships. Once ships had put into port and often stayed there for several weeks allowing time for repairs and maintenance. The sailors went ashore and were entertained. The industries and jobs that accumulated added to the prosperity of the city, but a container ship or a tanker can be in and out in a few hours and, as a result, most of those dependent trades withered and died. Now, even though a larger tonnage of goods is handled by the docks, the benefit to the fabric of the city is far less.

Faced with a depression and a change in status it has been difficult for even the best of modern architects to provide buildings which are unusually lively, ingenious and beautiful, particularly in a climate which has so often reacted against modern architecture.

No one knows what the future holds, but the past is still there in Liverpool, a splendid panorama from many generations which is a rich heritage well worth caring for and, indeed, boasting about.

Pre-nineteenth century architecture

1   **Stanlawe Grange**
     13th century and later
     Aigburth Hall Avenue,
     Grassendale, L19

This is possibly the oldest
remaining building in Liverpool.
The cruck building probably dates
from 1291 and has red
standstone walls. Modifications
have occured in the 15th, 16th
and 17th centuries and in 1967
an architect, David Brock,
converted it into two houses, one
for his own occupation. A
romantic restoration which brings
out the atmosphere of the past.

2   Speke Hall

Largely complete by 1598

Speke Hall Road, Speke, L25

Eight miles south of Liverpool, rather too near the airport. The house is framed-up in timber with an in-fill of plaster and was formerly surrounded by a dry ditch and approached over a stone bridge. A porch leads to an oblong inner court. The panelling in the fine baronial great hall is said to have been brought by the first owner, Sir Edward Norris, from the palace of the King of Scotland after the fatal battle of Flodden Field. There is an inscription on the house, 'This work, twenty yards long, was wholly built by EN 1598' but, except for the east range of the courtyard, the bulk of the house is early 16th century. Much of the interior is Victorian, like the insertion of some fireplaces, wall panelling and ceiling treatment, but lively and appropriate and carried out with confidence. The building has been well restored by the National Trust.

3   Tuebrook House

1615

Tuebrook, West Derby Road, L13

A small Lancashire Jacobean house carved with the date and the initials of John Mercer. It is a two storey building of brick with red sandstone dressings and has two wings which project slightly from the centrepiece. A charming example of the period well maintained.

4   Old School House, Walton

17th century

Walton Village, Walton, L4

This once charming early house faces onto the churchyard, but now, with its windows protected by wire mesh, it has sunk to the vandal-attacked level of much of Walton. A two-storey house, built of sandstone rubble with ashlar quoins, roofed with twin gables, set in a wooded landscape, it could be delightful.

5   Ancient Chapel of Toxteth

c1618 later altered

The corner of Park Road and Dingle Lane, Toxteth, L8

Probably built by Edward Aspinall in about 1618 during the reign of James I, it became a Unitarian church and has always held an association with the Dissenters. The early settlers at Toxteth had Puritan sympathies at a time when that did not separate them from the Established Church, and it is interesting to note that it was a Roman Catholic, Sir Richard Molyneux of Sefton, who granted them the land on which to build a chapel and a school house beside the little stream over which Park Road now runs. The interest is more historical than architectural. Restored and considerably modified in 1774 with a porch added in 1841. It contains some good 18th century furnishings.

6 Croxteth Hall

1702

Croxteth Hall Lane and Flint Drive, West Derby, L12

Croxteth Hall was begun by Sir Richard Molyneux about 1575 but little remains of the original structure. The impressive and most important part of the Hall is the west wing constructed between 1702 and 1714. Built of brick, it has classical stone dressings which are painted in the traditional Liverpool manner. When this fashion first started is not known but painted stone can be seen in Rodney Street and throughout the Georgian terraces of the city. It had the advantage of preserving the masonry in a damp, soot-laden atmosphere so it probably began in the 19th century. The west facade stands on a terrace pierced by oval lights and, approached by a noble flight of stairs; the entrance and the main rooms form a piano nobile in the Italian style. Stone quoins suggest an early 18th century date and the main windows are surmounted by alternate triangular and segmental pediments. However, their rhythm is strange with a narrower wall spacing between the two end ones. Perhaps this was dictated by earlier remains. It has been rectified on the parapet whose rhythm, as a result, pays little respect to the window spacing below. The stables were built by Caryll Molyneux between 1678 and 1706, and a small portion of the original Elizabethan house survives at the back. The charming dairy was designed by Eden Nesfield and built between 1861 and 1870. All the buildings are now in public ownership and may be visited.

7 Woolton Hall

1704 and later

Adjoining St Julie's School, Speke Road, Woolton, L25

Built by the son of Sir Richard Molyneux of Croxteth Hall and designed by an unknown architect of no great ability, this red sandstone Palladian villa was later extended by Robert Adam towards the end of the century. The result is an unsatisfactory mishmash of parts, some ill-proportioned and not coming together to form a coherent whole. In many ways the best elevation is that facing the school. It has a fine pediment filled with carved trophies, but below it the window spacing is odd with a string course placed high up, forming a sill to the top windows. They are strangely arranged with only two below the pediment leaving a solid centre to the building which should have contained a void. Notice the large expanse of wall between the upper and lower windows. This continues across the front elevation where circular plaques are inserted unconvincingly to try to fill the space. The three floors of fenestration in the slightly recessed centre of the main front bear no relationship to the wings. It is as though newer facades were added by Adams' office to a jumble of rooms that lay behind and the resultant facades could never be satisfactory. To make matters worse a large, ungainly porte-cochére was built in front of the main door in the 1860s, useful in providing a covered approach and an ample terrace on its roof, but otherwise out of character. Inside there are some rooms, including the Octagon Room, that may have been designed by Adams' office.

8   Old Bluecoat School

1717-25

School Lane, off Church Street, L1

This is the ancient gem of Liverpool, built slightly later than the west front of Croxteth Hall and with similarities, but much more carefully ordered and well proportioned. Stately and crisp Queen Anne style with a pleasant contrast between pointed dark brickwork and painted stone quoins and dressings. An extremely elegant building in the heart of the city, its tree lined courtyard and secluded rooms provide a haven for artists and art lovers. It provides an art gallery close to the main shops and has sculptors' workshops at the back with sculpture dotted about the garden, and a design centre shop. It had been founded in 1708 by benefactors who wished to provide a school in which to 'teach poor children to read, write and cast accounts, and to instruct them in the principles and doctrines of the Established Church'. Building of the present structure began in 1717 and it was complete by 1725, costing nearly £2,300. The architect is unknown but the name of Thomas Ripley, architect of the Old Customs House, has been put forward with some conviction. For a while, from 1910, this splendid building became the home of the Liverpool University School of Architecture through the munificence of William Lever, later first Lord Leverhulme. Lever wanted to turn the place into a great centre for the arts, with concert room, exhibition gallery and studios for artists, but the 1914-1918 war came and after that he never revived his scheme, the School of Architecture moving up to Brownlow Hill. The Bluecoat building was extensively damaged during the blitz but has been carefully restored and renovated.

9   Town Hall
1749 reconstructed 1807
Castle Street, L1
Architects: John Wood the Younger of Bath, James Wyatt and John Foster Jr

A classical gem of architecture closes the vista on Castle Street. John Wood's building was Liverpool's third town hall, a graceful classical structure in stone. The city fathers originally wanted to get the services of John Wood the Elder and they persuaded Mrs Clayton to intervene. She lived in Clayton Hall, a house which once stood where now stands the Clayton Square Shopping Precinct. She went to Bath and the elder Wood told her he was too busy, but he would prevail upon his son to do the job. All went well, with the younger architect taking up residence in Liverpool and producing an elegant building with fine interiors, but his dome was too squat and not raised on a drum so that the central hall was poorly lit. The city was embarrassed, but somewhat relieved when the building was gutted by fire in 1795. James Wyatt was called in to reconstruct the Town Hall, adding the Corinthian portico on its triple arched rusticated base and the impressive dome on its high drum. Wood's work can still be seen best on the rear facade from the small square behind the Town Hall, elegant and fine etched. Wyatt's additions add impressiveness to the main facade. The interior merits a visit. It has a gracious entrance hall, staircase and state apartments. Reception rooms of matchless beauty show Wyatt in his most mature style. John Foster collaborated in the work and must have been responsible for much of the execution. It should be noted that this building was intended to be used solely for ceremonial purposes, like the mansion houses at York and London. Most English town halls combine the dual purpose of providing for civic receptions and acting as municipal offices. Part of the ground floor was remodelled by Thomas Shelmerdine to form a grand Council Chamber. The whole building has recently been beautifully restored to its true civic splendour.

10 Church of St James

1774-75

On the corner of Upper Parliament Street and St James Place, L8

Architect: Cuthbert Bisbrowne

The land was presented by Lord Sefton and the church, which cost £3,000, was paid for by 27 shareholders – not an unusual procedure in those days. Picton describes it as 'a plain brick building, altogether out of the pale of criticism. Its square tower, and the small semicircular headed windows by which it is lighted, give something of a quaint Norman character to the structure'. Thus it is a dull church whose sole claim to prominence lies in the fact that it contains the earliest recorded remaining structure in cast iron in Britain. This in itself makes it important because cast and wrought iron were to revolutionise the architecture and engineering of the 19th century and here we see, in embryo, the start of the giant leap into vast light fireproof prefabricated structures which have transformed the appearance of Europe and America. Early cast iron columns support the gallery inside this church. These are predated by those in the Church of St Anne, in St Anne's Street, Liverpool, which was built in 1772 but has now been demolished, leaving St James as the earliest extant example. The columns are quatrefoil clusters, some 9ft high (2·74m) and 5in (12·7cm) in diameter, made in a single casting. The chancel is a late 19th century addition. The church was declared redundant and was supposed to be cared for against the ravages of vandals by the Redundant Churches Fund, now the Churches Conservation Trust. How wonderful it would be if it could be converted into a museum of iron architecture in whose development Liverpool has played such a significant part. However, it now looks as though the Trust is abrogating its responsibility, disliking the task of caring for threatened city centre churches. Several institutions have shown some interest in the building, but, at the time of writing, nothing has been done. It must be cared for and properly restored because this is an historical, architectural and engineering monument of the greatest importance.

11 Liverpool Institute High School for Girls

1785-90 Now Blackburne House Centre for Women
1994 Blackburne Place, off Hope Street, L1
Architects of the conversion: Maggie Pickles and Gladys Martinez
with Danielle Pacaud as consultant

Built originally as a large private house, it has a portico of four graceful Ionic columns, brick built with curved bows at the rear. The school was founded in 1844 and, over the years the house was converted. The front facing Hope Street is much later, dating from 1874 and designed in the style of the French Renaissance with its big, almost overpowering roof. In 1994 a woman client commissioned two women architects to convert the building into a centre for the high-quality training of women in technology; a most interesting project that continued the educational process begun in the original school. Like much of the work now going on in Liverpool, this was an interior scheme carried out within the fabric of an older building so that the public in general are not aware of the work that has gone on. But the whole idea of finding a new and appropriate use for old buildings is admirable, especially when it is done, as in this case, with such verve and good taste. In particular, the way in which natural daylight was brought into the original building, is continued in the conversion. In the words of the architects, 'Our design explores this approach further, revealing qualities of chiaroscuro in the sequence of spaces through the building. With the manipulation of surfaces, planes and volumes, serenity and intensity are intensified, details and hidden geometries uncovered'.

12 Roman Catholic Church of St Peter

1788
Seel Street, L1

This is the oldest Roman Catholic church in the city. A small building faced in stucco, its doorway containing attractive fluted Doric columns with a dated entablature. It was opened for worship on 7 September 1788 and was originally called the Seel Street Chapel, perhaps so as not to confuse it with the parish church of St Peter which then stood in Church Street. The nave has a contemporary gallery on three sides supported on cast iron columns, an early example of this form of construction. The chancel was added in 1843. After the Second World War the church was run by the Polish community, but, with their numbers shrunk, they found it impossible to keep it running and, at the time of writing, it is redundant.

13   Holy Trinity Church

1794-1911

Between Church Road North and Prince Alfred Street, Wavertree, L15

Architects: John Hope, Professor Sir Charles Reilly

In 1911, Charles Reilly, Professor of Architecture at Liverpool, removed the side galleries and cleverly slotted a new chancel into this 18th century church and it is undoubtedly this chancel, with its beautiful and delicate Greek Revival detailing and its Renaissance organisation of space, that is the main attraction. Even the old tower is buttressed to give it an obelisk effect. At its base he has placed a circular vaulted baptistery. Every detail is considered and the work shows Reilly at his best.

14   Houses in Rodney Street, Mount Street
      & Hope Street

Late 18th & early 19th century

Rodney Street, Mount Street & Hope Street, L1

Georgian urban architecture at its best. There is no coordinated design, no long composed terraces like Bath, Bloomsbury or Edinburgh, but instead a series of well mannered Georgian houses which stand side by side in harmony, each displaying its unique doorway, some with fine delicately traced fanlights, others with Greek, Roman or Renaissance classical porticoes. It must be pointed out that the word 'Georgian' in this book refers to a style and not to a royal house. The style continued to be used in Liverpool into the early years of Victoria's reign. Rodney Street is Liverpool's Harley Street; once the province of doctors and consultants, now architects and engineers have edged in together with the Liverpool John Moores University. A fine street of Georgian houses dating mainly from the end of the 18th century and the beginning of the 19th century. 'The doctors have taste,' wrote Reilly, 'there is no doubt about it. They have chosen and made their own the one street in Liverpool in which we ordinary mortals would most like to live. Its character is at once definite and elegant'. Gladstone was born in No 62 Rodney Street. There are a few architectural bad teeth but not sufficient to mar the charming smile of this pleasant street, a charm which spreads into the adjoing Georgian Mount Street and Faulkner Street. The Georgian houses extend up Mount Street into Hope Street where there are several good examples. One must remember that this development of Georgian architecture once swept in a broad half-circle around Liverpool and some of the finest examples were to be found at the northern end in Shaw Street.

Nineteenth century architecture

15 **Lyceum**
1800-02
At the bottom of Bold Street, L1
Architect: Thomas Harrison

Thomas Harrison (1744-1829) was a Yorkshire architect who did most of his work in the North West, particularly in Chester where he designed the county courts and other buildings in the castle. In Liverpool he designed, in addition to the Lyceum, the tower of St Nicholas, the old Jewish Synagogue in Seel Street, and the original building for the Athenaeum. The Lyceum is an impressive if somewhat heavy handed example of Harrison's monumental style. In spite of its six Ionic columns on the Bold Street facade, it possesses more of the masculine strength of the Doric order than the feminine delicacy of Ionic. The building, once a gentleman's club, had an impressive circular library inadequately top lit, housing what is claimed to have been the oldest proprietary circulating library in Europe. Although the Lyceum was founded in 1759, the Public News & Coffee Room, with its library, was not opened until 1802. The idea of having a meeting place where merchants could discuss business and, in particular, the movement of shipping, was modelled on the London coffee-house clubs. The weather vane placed on the roof was once of considerable importance to maritime merchants and ship owner members as it gave warning of the approach of their ships in the Mersey.

The building has now been cleaned and restored by Rodney Hutchinson, who has lovingly handled this fine structure, removing the clutter on the roof and restoring the building more nearly to its original shape, and converting the interior with its large circular room into what must be the most elegant post office in Britain.

16 Heywood's Bank

1800

Later Martins and now solicitors' offices
Brunswick Street off Castle Street, L1

Built as a private bank for Arthur Heywood, it was later
acquired by Martins Bank showing their remarkable taste in
always buying or building good architecture. It was later taken
over by Barclays. It has a serene five bay Classical facade in
ashlar with a rusticated ground floor and blind arcading, very
elegant and well-proportioned with a minimum of decoration
and quite austere.

17 Union Newsroom

1800

Duke Street, Slater Street, L1
Architect: John Foster the Elder

Now used as offices by the Bibby Line, the only
major shipping company to retain its head office
in Liverpool, this was the city's first rate-supported
public library in a city that pioneered the idea. It is
a stately, grave late Classical building, well
proportioned with a pedimented facade
containing a Venetian window onto Slater Street.
Like the best buildings of its period and much in
the style of Wyatt, its detail is elegant and refined
and its mouldings of slight projection with the
result that it needs some contemplation before its
qualities are evident.

18   Nelson Memorial

1807-15
Exchange Flags,
behind the Town Hall, L1
Designer: Matthew Cotes Wyatt
Sculptor: Richard Westmacott RA

Designed more to represent the rising maritime prowess of Liverpool than to commemorate the death of Nelson, this large sculptural set-piece is, through its sheer size and bulk, as much a work of architecture as of sculpture. Instigated two years after the death of the naval hero, it was designed to be placed in the commercial centre of the city by a young sculptor, Matthew Cotes Wyatt (1777-1862) with Liverpool connections. In the event, William Roscoe, whose home, Allerton Hall [19] is illustrated, and who was the chief instigator of the project, wanted to use a famous London sculptor. As a result, Richard Westmacott (1775-1856) was called in to complete the design and execute it. It is a large circular monument in bronze on a marble base where four chained prisoners sit in dejection. These may also be a subtle allusion to Roscoe's hatred of the slave trade. The setting in which it was designed has now been destroyed and the banal background of Derby House does little to enhance its dignity.

19 Allerton Hall

Mainly early 18th century, completed c1810-12

Between Allerton Road, Calderstones and Mather Avenue, L18

An Elizabethan house, partly rebuilt in the early 18th century, with early 19th century alterations including the provision of a library and music room. For a while, it was the home of the Liverpool merchant prince, William Roscoe (1753-1831), who fell in love with the Italian Renaissance and, although he never visited Italy, wrote excellent books on the life of Pope Leo X and Lorenzo de Medici. At this time, the wealthy traders of the city liked to feel that the mantle of the once flourishing commercial city of Florence had fallen upon their shoulders and any depiction of Florentine life was attractive. 'The merchant princes of Liverpool are living facts of modern enterprise' wrote the Liverpool Mercury in 1857. Roscoe sent agents to Italy to buy illuminated manuscripts and paintings, in particular the Primitives which now form so important a part of the Walker Art Gallery collection. The front of his hall was very much in this spirit although the inspiration stemmed from Venice. It is a large Palladian facade built in local red sandstone with a slightly projecting central portico of unfluted Ionic columns, not unusual in the North West, and a plain pediment. The wings also have a slight projection defined by quoins. The ground floor actually drops into a plinth upon which rests a rusticated base with a plain string course. The portico and the piano nobile with large pedimented windows rise from this. It is, in essence, the stately country house of the 18th century, but largely done in the early 19th century. Poor Roscoe was not to enjoy it for long. By 1816 he was bankrupt and had to leave but, being an honourable man, he insisted on paying, in time, as many of his creditors as possible. However, it is important to realise it was largely due to men of taste like Roscoe that Liverpool was to produce so much fine commercial architecture. The patronage of the merchants who knew what they wanted, appreciated the work of good architects and had the means to carry out their wishes, has produced a city of architecture without parallel in England.

20 Seymour Terrace
c1810-28
Seymour Street, behind Lime Street Station, L3
A neat terrace of three-storey late Georgian style houses in red brick recently lovingly restored by Inner City Enterprises and converted into offices. They step in pairs up the slight gradient of the street. The backs have been totally rebuilt but the original facades have been retained. The regular rows of chimney stacks create a rhythm sadly missing in modern terrace housing.

21 Church of Our Lady & St Nicholas Tower
1811-15
On the corner of Chapel Street and George's Dock Gate, L3
Architect: Thomas Harrison
Nave rebuilt 1952, Architect: Edward C Butler

It is difficult to put a date to this building because it has so often been rebuilt, altered and changed. The original church was part of the oldest ecclesiastical foundation in Liverpool, forming a chapel of rest in the parish of Walton. On 24 June 1699 an Act of Parliament was passed establishing a new parish of Liverpool and empowering the corporation to build a church. In 1746 a new spire was added and, in 1759, a coast defence battery of 14 guns placed in the cemetery to protect the port from the threat of attack by French privateers.

In 1774 the church was almost entirely rebuilt. However, the church tower was not strong so that, when the bells were rung vigorously, the whole thing suddenly collapsed on a Sunday morning, crushing and killing 23 girls from the Moorfields Charity School on 11 February 1810. After this tragedy, Thomas Harrison, the Chester architect, was called in to design a new tower. This fine structure, in the Gothic style, some 120ft (36·5m) high, was surmounted by an elegant lantern rising a further 60ft at a cost of £22,000. For a Classical architect this is quite an advanced example of Gothic Revival, considering the date of its design. It is mature Perpendicular and has an elevated lantern buttressed from the base of the tower pinnacles. At the time and for many years after it dominated the skyline of the port. During the Second World War the nave was largely destroyed by bombs and had to be rebuilt in an emaciated Gothic manner. Like so many urban churches in the city centres of western cities, this one is now swamped by high buildings, in particular by the adjacent block of the Atlantic Towers Hotel.

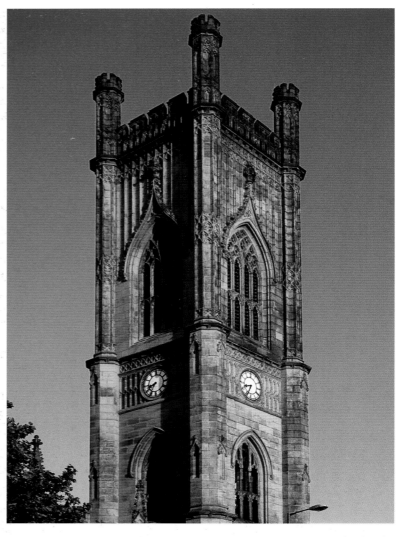

22 Duke's Warehouse

1811, now demolished

Duke's Dock, Wapping, L1

This is one of the greatest losses for it had stood intact and undamaged until the 1960s when, with the closing of the South Docks to shipping, it became redundant and was demolished. I shall list a number of buildings whose retention and preservation would have greatly enhanced the townscape of Liverpool and whose loss is thus particularly sad. Built by the Duke of Bridgewater as the terminal for goods shipped down his canal for trans-shipment at Liverpool, it rose through six storeys from a stone rusticated base, a great brick classical structure with a pediment in the middle of its main facade. From the canal two arched caverns led barges into its interior. Had it been saved it would have made a splendid compliment to the bulk of the Albert Dock Warehouses facing it across the waters of the docks. Its method of construction was equally important. Its interior was supported on cast iron beams between brick cross walls which acted as fire checks and the top floors were supported on giant elephant beams of cast iron, curved over like immense tusks.

23 St Luke's Church

Foundation 1802, built 1811-31

St Luke's Place, Berry Street, L1

Architects: John Foster the Elder and John Foster, Jr

The church was originally by the elder Foster, but work was suspended and not resumed until 1826, when the younger Foster submitted a new design. This is Foster's essay in cardboard Gothic, so out of character with his usual heavy Classical style that credit must surely go to his chief assistant, Mr Edwards. The handling of the chancel was interesting because it was well in advance of the ideas later advocated by the Ecclesiological Society, although one must remember that the shift from congregational worship to a focus on devotional worship was already being discussed by the Anglicans. Its tower, a finger pointing to the sky, closes the vista at the top of Bold Street and Renshaw Street; a familiar landmark and a valuable point of identity. Reilly eulogized about this tower. 'Who, returning at night from the make-believe of our theatres, has not appreciated its far greater theatricality.'

The church was ripped apart by bombs during World War II and its gutted nave and chancel have been retained as a memorial to the blitz on Liverpool.

24 St George's Church

1812-14

St Domingo Road, Heyworth Street, Everton, L5

Architects: Thomas Rickman and John Cragg

This is an elegant Gothic iron church of outstanding importance, constructed within an external casing of stone. Its significance lies in the fact that it was probably the earliest example of the use of large scale prefabricated dry construction. All the pieces of this church were made in the factory of John Cragg, taken to the site by horse and cart, and bolted into position. In building construction it was one of the great advances to be made in the century, a milestone in architectural construction. Here was a building where, once the moulds were made, as many casting could be produced as was required. The building could be constructed rapidly and cheaply and could be occupied almost immediately without the need for the walls to dry out – a lengthy procedure with stone and brick buildings. The tie-beams are later additions inserted to prevent the outer wall of stone from bulging. Rickman, whom the Bishop of Chester called 'a very ingenious deserving man', gave evidence to the Church Commissioners of the value of this form of construction. Referring to the patterns, the most important items in construction, he wrote, 'If only one church was to be erected and the patterns then became useless, they might perhaps cost £150; but as many churches are to be built, the windows and other things being carefully prepared to be generally useful, the cost of patterns might be reduced to a trifle for each church'. Undoubtedly, this church fostered the rapid expansion of the export of prefabricated iron buildings from the Port of Liverpool.

25 The Hermitage

c1812

St Michael's Church Road, Toxteth, L8

The Hermitage is one of a number of houses in the hamlet of the iron founder, John Cragg and, as a result, items of cast iron are to be found everywhere; in the columns supporting porches, in gate posts, window frames, fireplaces and stairs. The village, with its cast iron church, is virtually a museum of early 19th century iron architecture. Cragg was the owner of what later was to be known as the Mersey Steel and Iron Company with works in Grafton Street. It was established as a private forge for the manufacture of iron from scrap and grew to become a large and prosperous business. Cragg had cast iron on the brain and used it wherever he could.

26 Church of St Michael in the Hamlet

1814-15

St Michael's Church Road, Toxteth, L8

Architects: Thomas Rickman and John Cragg

The second essay in prefabricated cast iron construction built in Cragg's own hamlet. It is a simpler solution than St George's, Everton, but many of the patterns were reused on this church. Although the main walls are built of brick as a cladding, externally the use of cast iron is more in evidence. Finials, parapets, and copings are all in this material, and the cast iron frame is exposed externally at clerestory level. Spanning the iron frame in the roof are slabs of Welsh slate. Rickman claimed that churches of this type could be built for an average of £6,000. St George's had cost £9,000, but this was probably due to the extensive use of stone on the outside.

Since it was originally designed, several alterations have been carried out including a widening of the north aisle in 1900 and the placing of a wooden reredos which obscured the lower panes of the iron east window. This reredos has now been removed and placed under the tower.

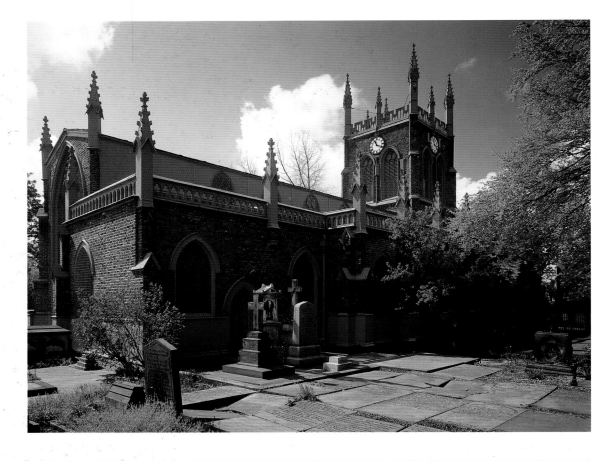

27 Greenbank House

c1815

Greenbank Lane, opposite the end of Greenbank Park, L17

The home of the Rathbone family from 1787, a hotbed of political and social reform. The main block is a graceful marriage of Georgian and Gothic styles, but the lace-like cast iron screen on the garden facade is its most charming feature. This probably dates from about 1815 and is characteristic of the extensive use of decorative cast iron work in Liverpool, a style which spread to the Southern States of America and the colonies in Australia and New Zealand. In 1964 the building was converted by the author into a university club for staff and students.

28 Royal Institution

1814-17

Colquitt Street, L1

Architect: Edmond Aikin

Originally a gentleman's house built for Thomas Parr the banker, the building was turned into the Institution in 1814 when the stone porticoed entrance was added by Edmond Aikin. This portico became a prototype for many later built to adorn the facades of the houses of rich merchants. The building consists of a central block, almost square, with wings on each side in the Palladian manner, unusual in town houses. Notice how the rhythm of the window openings has been maintained where no opening lights were required, especially down the side elevations. The Institution was incorporated in 1822 by Royal Charter for 'the promotion of Literature, Science and the Arts' by academic schools; by public lectures; by the encouragement of societies; by the collection of books, specimens of art, natural history etc.; and by providing a laboratory and philosophical apparatus' – noble sentiments, indeed, by the citizens of a city that prided itself on its cultural taste. William Roscoe opened the place with a lecture on 25 November 1817. Inside there had been provided a spacious reading room, a lecture theatre to hold 500, committee rooms and classrooms with, on the first floor, a large room for the use of the Literary and Philosophical Society of Liverpool. There was a spacious exhibition room for the Liverpool Academy and another held a splendid display of casts of the Greek Elgin and Aegina marbles, research on which had largely been the work of Liverpool architects steeped in Greek culture, including John Foster Junior who, with Cockerell, had brought to England the Aegina Marbles. There is a platform on the roof which was used as an observatory. The cultural tradition was continued by the Department of Extra Mural Studies of the University of Liverpool which occupied the building, but now, sadly, that appropriate use has been discontinued.

29 Wellington Rooms

1815

Mount Pleasant, L1

Architect: Edmond Aikin

These assembly rooms, described as a 'house of mirth and revelry', were erected by public subscription after the Battle of Waterloo. The facade consists of a circular Greek temple attached to an ashlar wall, an adaptation of the Choragic Monument of Lysicrates at Athens which was illustrated by Stuart and Revett in their influential book *The Antiquities of Athens*. There was a porch on the west side provided for the setting down of sedan chairs. The circular portico was originally open, but on being found to be too draughty, the inter-columnations were walled up – a sad disfigurement! The building has a splendid ballroom, measuring 80ft by 37ft (24 x11m), a card room and a supper room. 'The whole are appropriated to the amusements of the upper classes of society, as subscription balls, assemblies and occasionally fancy dress balls.'

30 St John's Market

1820-22, now demolished

Elliot Street and once Great Charlotte Street, L1

Architect: John Foster Jr

Gone but not forgotten. Designed by Foster like some Early Christian basilica; a great hall with a trussed timber roof supported on incredibly tall thin cast iron columns, each rising some 25ft (7·6m), it comprised a sort of nave with double broad aisles. It must have been an impressive interior. This very large building, which had eight spacious entrances, was commissioned by the Corporation at a cost of £35,000 and begun in August 1820. It was opened to the public in February 1822. It has now been replaced by a modern shopping centre which is wrapped around a new market hall.

31 Roman Catholic Church of St Patrick

1821-27

Park Place, L8

Architect: John Slater

An aggressively solid structure in brick and painted stone, placed high above the street. It is very much in the classical tradition of Liverpool. However, the two quite absurd large Greek Doric porticoes tucked into the corners of the Greek Cross plan look as though they have been purchased from a DIY store and stuck onto the church. In front of the building stands the well-executed effigy of St Patrick, in his episcopal robes, in the act of benediction. It came as a present from Dublin where it had once decorated the front of the offices of the St Patrick Insurance Company. The old high altar was designed by JF Bentley and FX Velarde probably did the baptistery.

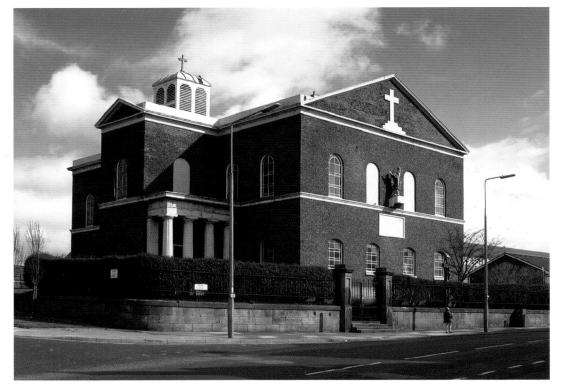

32 Statue of George III
1822
Monument Place on the junction of London Road and Pembroke Place, L3
Sculptor: Richard Westmacott RA

It was originally designed to go on a site in Great George Square to celebrate the Golden Jubilee of George III. A foundation stone was laid there in October 1809 but was later moved to Monument Place where its future is now being debated. It was erected in 1822, two years after the king had died, so it became a monument to him. Costing nearly £4,000, it is a fine equestrian statue cast in bronze raised on a high stone pedestal. Westmacott at his best, it portrays the king, dressed like a Roman emperor in an ancient toga and sitting astride a splendid mount. Liverpool is remarkable for its equestrian statues, having more than any other city outside the capital. This one, a piece of architecture in itself, was inspired by Roman precedent, being modelled on the statue of Marcus Aurelius which still stands on Capital Hill in Rome.

33 St Andrew's Presbyterian Church
1823
Rodney Street, L1
Architect: John Foster, Jr

Once described as 'an ornament to the town', this was a somewhat stumpy twin-towered stone facade attached as a screen to the stucco body of the church. The Ionic portico is recessed, framed by solid wings and a heavy ballustraded attic which form a base for the saucer-domed towers. Each turret of these square towers had a window on each side, surrounded by eight Corinthian columns with full entablature and pediment which somewhat reduced the effect of the domes. The detailing throughout is Greek and the interior meeting hall had panelled galleries supported upon graceful columns. However the building was very much an elegant front with cheap back and sides, originally faced in plain brick but later stuccoed to give some 'appearance of congruity to the whole'. It was obviously done on the cheap and not one of Foster's best buildings. As I write, it seems even less inspiring, having been gutted by fire and one of its towers removed to render the structure 'safe'. However, there is still a hope that the Liverpool John Moores University may acquire it and use its as both an extension and a frontispiece to the Library and Learning Resource Centre [226]. It is possible to continue the main axis of the Resource Centre in a straight line through the back of the old church to its monumental facade. What a splendid composition this would make and a tribute to the architectural endeavours of the new university!

34   Houses in Abercromby Square

1824

Abercromby Square, University Precinct, L1

Architect for the plan: John Foster the Elder with William Gates & Charles Eyes

The plan was presented in 1800, but work probably began in 1824. Named after Sir Ralph Abercromby (1734-1801), the British general who commanded the British troops in the Mediterranean and who defeated the French at Alexandria in Egypt, dying from wounds he received in the battle, this is the first of the Liverpool residential squares modelled on Bloomsbury. It occupied some three and a half acres of land part of which was formerly a lake. The houses, which line three sides of the square, were once the homes of prosperous Liverpool merchants. Each family had access to the spacious tree-planted square in which stands a small circular garden house surrounded by a cast iron trellis. The central garden area was secured by railings and locked gates which could only be opened by the owners of the houses. It was thus a private domain. These houses may appear elegant, serene and confident, but they were also designed for defence. Some of the merchants who now moved out of the town centre and built themselves Georgian-style houses on the ring of hills around Liverpool had experienced the destructive effects of riots on property in the town when shops and other premises had been attacked by mobs and destroyed. The new builders were to take no chances. The houses are separated from the pavement by a high iron railing and a deep dry ditch, difficult to cross. The ditches of the houses in Abercromby Square had vertical scarp and counterscarp walls modelled on contemporary military architecture. This allowed light to enter the barred windows of the basement but prevented a mob storming the building. The only approach to each house was up a flight of stone steps, never an easy direction of attack, and against a heavy, solid wooden door. The only window in their line of attack was a fanlight high above the door. In earlier contrast, most of the houses in Rodney Street, built before the threat of mob attack materialised, spring straight from the pavement. The regular Georgian terrace houses of Abercromby Square are now used by the University and the far side of the square, which once contained John Foster's church of St Catherine, has now been demolished to make way for the University Senate House [218]. Its fine Ionic stone portico could have been retained and incorporated into the facade of the new building.

35   St James's Cemetery

1825-29

St James's Road, below the Anglican Cathedral, L1

Architect: John Foster Jr

A 'city of the dead', the cemetery was created from a disused stone quarry and is now a romantic arborial setting somewhat disfigured by 20th century litter. Great ramps, wide enough to take funeral carriages, their roadways protected by raised walls to prevent those carriages from falling off the edge, served to convey the funeral processions to its sunken floor. Over a hundred catacombs were hollowed in its sandstone walls and tunnels pierced the rock. This setting on an immense scale is one of the most powerful and picturesque spectacles in Liverpool, awe inspiring in its mouldering decay. It was modelled on the cemetery of Père-la-Chaise in Paris. St James's Cemetery contains John Foster's memorial to the member of parliament, William Huskisson, who was knocked down and killed by the steam engine, Rocket, at the opening of the Liverpool to Manchester railway in 1830, just as he was attempting to heal a longstanding quarrel with the Duke of Wellington. John Gibson's marble effigy was once tight-pinned within the dome structure, clad heroically in a Roman toga and visible only from below. Now, even that has had to been removed for safekeeping.

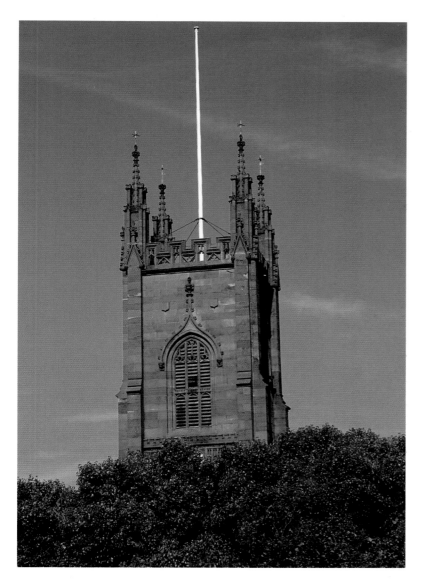

36   Church of St Mary, Tower
1828-32
Walton Village, Walton L4
Architect: John Broadbent

Until 1699 this was the parish church of Liverpool but little of the original church remains, it having been rebuilt and restored on many occasions. John Broadbent built the fine tower between 1828 and 1832. He was a local architect, pupil of Thomas Rickman the author of the famous book on the origin of the styles of Gothic architecture, so Broadbent had a good grounding in the Gothic style. The year before he had designed St Augustine's at Everton. Sadly, he was to die young. This tower is in the Perpendicular style, its upper windows dressed with delicate carved ogee mouldings and the set-back buttresses with their tall pinnacles further accentuate the verticality of the design. The north side of the church dates from 1840 and the south aisle chapel was built in 1911. It was again rebuilt after bomb damage by Quiggin & Gee, omitting the aisles and giving the interior an appearance vaguely reminiscent of a cinema.

37   Oratory, a Greek Temple
1829
St James's Cemetery, adjoining the Anglican Cathedral, L1
Architect: John Foster Jr

This mortuary chapel of St James is a miniature Greek temple in the Doric style, the result of John Foster Junior's travels to Asia Minor with Charles Robert Cockerell between 1809 and 1816 when Foster was able to study and sketch ancient Greek architecture at first hand. The lovely little building, carefully restored and cleaned, is now somewhat dwarfed by the Anglican Cathedral. Placed on its miniature acropolis, the Oratory once crowned the picturesque deep hollow chasm of St James's cemetery. The building is of brick core faced with grey gritstone similar to that used on St George's Hall. The roof has stone slates and a coffered plaster ceiling. At each end there is a correct portico of six Greek Doric columns, with four internal Ionic columns supporting the ceiling. The interior is lit solely from a glass fanlight between these columns. In 1832 it was described as being 'in the very spirit and soul of the Greek school'. It epitomises the strong feeling for Greek architecture which arose in the minds of the more cultured Liverpool businessmen early in the 19th century and lingered on well into this century, largely through the influence of Sir Charles Reilly, in banks and office buildings and in the Liverpool Athenaeum.

38 Customs House

1828-39, now demolished
Canning Place, the Dock Road, L1
Architect: John Foster the Elder

With the Act of 1825, the Corporation decided to fill in the Old Dock and build a new Customs House on the site. The building was also to provide excise, post and dock offices. The architect was the senior John Foster, then Surveyor to the Corporation. It faced the Town Hall down the length of Castle Street and was the largest building in Liverpool at the time. Its south facade looked out over Canning and Salthouse Docks. Picton disliked it, remarking that 'sadness and gloom predominate to an almost painful degree', but then he also disliked the Albert Dock Warehouses, preferring 'a Greek temple, constructed in white marble, glistening under the blue sun of Athens, its mouldings encrusted with carving' away from the murky, moist atmosphere of Liverpool. We would now consider the Customs House most impressive, its sombre architecture without decoration or sculpture, appropriate to a northern commercial city and akin to the work of Thomas Harrison on the Castle at Chester. Each facade had an attached Ionic portico with a broad, plain Greek pediment, the columns being unfluted in the manner favoured by Harrison. The proportions were all correct, for Foster knew his Greek architecture better than anyone. The dome was sparse but impressive and Foster had wanted a peripheral colonnade but this had been omitted for economy's sake. There were few windows visible in the walls and the general impression was one of noble dignity. What a sad loss. It is recorded here because it need not have gone. Bombed during the blitz of the Second World War, its shell was largely intact and could have been restored although an alternate use would have been difficult. Its great stone bulk, larger than St George's Hall, would have formed a splendid compliment to the Albert Dock Warehouses opposite which it stood.

39 Church of St Bride

Commenced 1830
Percy Street, L8
Architect: Samuel Rowland

A classical Greek temple in the heart of Liverpool's Georgian residential area. The western Ionic portico has an impressive appearance of strength and stability and is very much in keeping with the contemporary stone houses in the street in spite of its being faced in painted stucco. Gore's directory of 1834 refers to it as 'another modern building in the Grecian style of architecture with a fine portico of columns 8ft 3in (2·5m) in diameter and in height 29ft 4in (8·9m) and with spacious accommodation, there being room for 1,400 persons including 400 sittings for the poor'. The interior was considerably changed by the Victorians.

40   Sudley Museum & Art Gallery
1830s
Mossley Hill Road and close to Mossley Hill Church, L18
A strange austere classical building handled by an unknown architect with some uncertainty, for the pieces do not fit well together. It consists of a plain ashlar two-storey block, the floor defined by a string course and the end facade having two projecting blocks. Between these the architect has inserted a classical portico on the ground floor only, so that it looks stunted. Even worse is the porticoed entrance which does not even rise to the height of the string course. As remarked later, the rich Liverpool merchants favoured two extremes of architecture, the flamboyant and the austere. This is in the latter style with window openings devoid of decoration; mere holes punched in the plain ashlar walling. The house, once belonging to the Holt family, is now a delightful art gallery of paintings and furniture which give a very good idea of the quality of life enjoyed by the rich in Liverpool in the 19th century.

41 Houses in Canning Street

1830s

Canning Street, L8

Canning Street is typical of many once fine Georgian streets which stretched across the hillside east of the Anglican Cathedral. The houses are regular and well proportioned and the streets wide and commodious. This is the famous 'Liverpool 8', once peopled by rich merchants and now the flats of artists, poets and students – a variegated cosmopolitan area of some character. The pattern continues along Percy Street [42], Huskisson Street [43], Catharine Street, Falkner Square [44] and Upper Parliament Street [79] to eventual oblivion in the twilight zones.

42 Houses in Percy Street

c1832

Percy Street, L8

Percy Street is Liverpool's little Edinburgh, two impressive terraces of stone with delicate carved Grecian detail and pleasing cast iron balconies. Its masonry architecture stands out in contrast to the normal brick construction of Liverpool Georgian. Possibly designed by John Foster Jr; it is certainly elegant enough to have come from his hand. A pair of stone Gothic houses is inserted in the street. One would have thought these an aesthetic intrusion but, because of the sympathetic use of similar stone and the careful detailing, they seem to fit in. Perhaps we have just got used to them!

43 Houses in Huskisson Street
c1833
Huskisson Street, L8

Cathedral Mansions are the earliest, stately stuccoed Regency style terrace houses with, now, a view of the Anglican Cathedral. Divided into flats, they have recently been well restored and look very impressive. The terrace block opposite St Bride's Church is also of this date.

44 Falkner Square
1835
Falkner Square, L8

An early example of the private square modelled on Bloomsbury. It was planted in 1835 and surrounded by iron railings and gate posts. The houses, terraces of elegant stuccoed Regency design set behind forest trees give it a peaceful character. This must once have been one of the most charming urban settings for residential life, combining a compactness of housing with the greenery of forest trees, particularly plane trees, bringing town and country together. Unfortunately there are modern intrusions in the area which, although of great social value, are totally lacking in an understanding of the setting.

45 Halifax House
1835 but possibly later
Brunswick Street, off Castle Street, L1

At first offices were opened in the rooms of private houses or warehouses and sometimes above shops. This is one of the earliest buildings designed exclusively as an office block, a new building type being developed in London and Liverpool at that time which was eventually to become the most important building type of the 20th century, dominating the skylines of European and American cities. This is a modest statement of three storeys with four bays of windows divided by Tuscan pilasters and a frieze of triglyphs and metopes, bringing a taste of classical refinement to a functional building type. Some early offices were designed like Florentine palaces, a trend encouraged by merchants like William Roscoe enamoured by the charms of that great Italian business centre, birthplace of modern banking, but in Liverpool the small window openings, adequate in the bright sunlight of Italy, provided inadequate internal lighting conditions in a sombre northern climate before the invention of the electric fluorescent lighting tube.

46 Mechanics' Institute or Liverpool Institute School
1835-37
Mount Street, L1
Architect: AH Holme

The original Institute is an impressive typical early 19th century building in the Liverpool Classical tradition. The result is somewhat heavy handed but noble, very much in keeping with the Georgian environs. The main stone facade has two storeys with a central Ionic portico and this is all that remains of the old school now that the conversion has been completed. Paul McCartney, one of the Beatles, was a schoolboy here and has backed a major scheme to convert the building into a new Liverpool Institute for the Performing Arts. The additions amount to an almost complete building which turns the corner into Pilgrim Street with a bold glass drum reminiscent of the prewar work in Germany of Eric Mendelsohn, or, indeed, of the Odeon cinemas of the 1930s. The new portion is sensitively handled, particularly in the way it is joined onto the old Institute building and all the materials that have been chosen are sympathetic with good matching masonry. The facade facing Upper Duke Street is well set back and boldly handled, its three floors each of six square windows in complete symmetry, emphasised by a tip-tilted roof that gives it an almost Chinese effect. In front a forum is laid out, a stage set to create a space that can be used by staff and students.

47 **Edge Hill Railway Station**
    1836
    Tunnel Road, Edge Hill, L7
Two storey sandstone buildings form the
station buildings of what is the first
passenger railway station in the world,
built as the terminus of the Liverpool to
Manchester Railway which was later
continued through deep stone cuttings and
tunnels to Lime Street Station. Built of plain
classical ashlar, the twin blocks flank the
up and down lines of the railway track.
There are extensions built in 1848. The
buildings were restored by British Rail in
1979 with the help of the Historic
Buildings Council.

48 **Church of St Anne**
    1836-37
    Aigburth Road, opposite Dundonald Road, L17
    Architects: Cunningham & Holme
This is an early example of the revival of
Norman church architecture with the result that,
although many of the details are admirable, the
overall effect is not very convincing. It lacks the
gravity and massive bulk of its original inspiration
and the result looks as though it has been cut
from thick cardboard, but it was difficult in the
19th century, with the constraints of cost and
building materials, to achieve a convincing
revival. It inspired criticism when it was built for
The Ecclesiologist called its west tower
'laughable'. Nowadays one might call it 'a
brave attempt'.

49   Gambier Terrace
      c1836
      Hope Street, L1
      Architect: probably John Foster Jr

Speculative housing in the grand Classical manner. The original intention was to extend this stone and stucco terrace to the full length of St James's Cemetery, but for financial reasons it had to be abandoned. Variegated colour schemes and indiscriminate painting have ruined the original unity but the grandeur of the conception is still apparent in the giant order of engaged Corinthian columns and the mall-like screen in stumpy Doric which links the two projecting wings. The line of buildings was later continued to Huskisson Street in yellow brick with a touch of French Renaissance, but to nothing like the original grand style.

50 Medical Institution

1836-37

Mount Pleasant, L1

Architect: Clark Rampling

The corner of Mount Pleasant and Hope Street was once the site of a bowling green and an inn where William Roscoe was born in 1753, his father being the innkeeper. This is now the site of the Medical Institution. Its origins can be traced back to 1779 when a group of enlightened Liverpool doctors formed the Liverpool Medical Library. Closely linked with the library was the Liverpool Medical Society formed in 1833 for the promotion of medical research and knowledge. As a result of this merger the doctors commissioned Clark Rampling to design a building. As the site was triangular, the architect had to fit his accommodation into that shape, skillfully inserting a lecture theatre on two floors, a central hall, a library, a museum and committee rooms, all ingeniously lit by glazed domes. This is a typical Liverpool Classical building with a recessed Ionic portico built on the curve of the street, a feature which adds considerably to its graceful appearance. It provides a good start to Georgian Hope Street.

51 Queen Insurance Building

1837-39

Dale Street, L1

Architect: Samuel Rowland

One of the few remnants of an earlier classical Dale Street, it was formerly the Royal Bank. The piano nobile has a giant Corinthian order embracing the centre section of two floors of white sash windows. A pierced balustrade and a delightful spiky royal coat-of-arms provide a lively silhouette on the skyline of the street. The building is scooped out to provide the Queen's Arcade, a peaceful haven from the bustle of the business street.

52 Rigby's Buildings

c1840

Dale Street, L1

One of the earlier buildings on Dale Street was refaced in the middle of the 19th century. Although the facade has the date 1726 inscribed on it, the decoration we see today dates from the time of the rebuilding. Its facade is modelled on an Italian palazzo but, because it had to come to terms with five floors of accommodation, its architect has had to solve some problems. He has broken the design down into three horizontal spaces, rusticating the wall surface on the two lower floors above the shops and putting his main windows at second floor level with alternate triangular and segmental pediments. He has then coupled the top floor windows. All this is rather un-Italian Renaissance but quite a good solution to the problem.

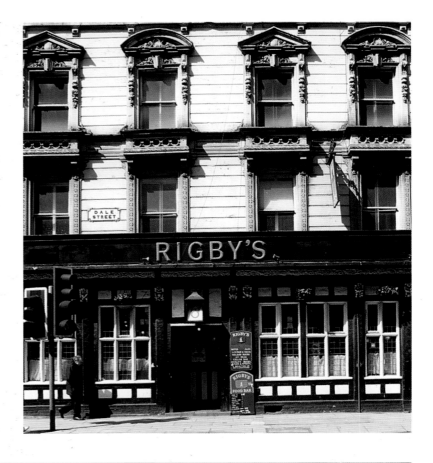

53 3-5 Castle Street

1839

Castle Street, L1

Architects: Grayson & Ould

A powerful six storey office building with a ground floor of polished red granite. There is a mosaic frieze over the first floor depicting sailing ships and an inscription 'British and Foreign Marine Insurance Company Limited', an indication of the growing strength of insurance in Liverpool in the 19th century. Outside London, Liverpool was to become the main insurance city of the country.

54   Warehouses

Warehouses abounded inland of the Dock Road and numerous examples could be found north and south of the Pier Head. For the most part, the merchants were conservative men building with traditional inflammable materials when manufacturers had already gone over to using noncombustible iron construction in the factories and mills of the North and Midlands. Many of the early warehouses were rather like tall houses and some contained the living accommodation of the merchant. They were also sited in the town and were a fire risk to other buildings. Goods had to be brought to them for storage and then again transported to the ships in the docks – a double process with the increased likelihood of pilfering and damage. Not until after fires had caused immense loss, and the Liverpool Warehouse Act of 1844 had been introduced, did merchants begin to substitute cast and wrought iron for timber columns and beams. The Albert Dock Warehouses [55] illustrate this development. Even so, many privately owned warehouses were slow to be changed right up to the end of the century. Gradually a new form of giant warehouse began to appear, towering above the Dock Road, giving a new scale to Liverpool. Sadly, most of these have now been demolished.

55 Albert Dock Warehouses

Designed 1839, opened 1845
South Docks, L1
Architects: Jesse Hartley and Phillip Hardwick

A monumental mass of warehouses constructed entirely of fire proof material. This is the first enclosed warehouse system built within the Liverpool Docks, designed so that ships could be berthed in the dock and could be loaded and unloaded directly from and to the surrounding warehouses. Few Victorian buildings can equal their size and splendour. They stand as massive monuments to the maritime prosperity of the Port of Liverpool. The cast iron columns which support the superstructure are modelled on Greek Doric prototypes, and are hollow drums, 12ft 6in (3·8m) in circumference and 15ft (4·5m) high. Encased within a wall of brick, five floors of the warehouses are supported on thinner iron columns between which span inverted iron Y-beams, pre-tensioned with wrought iron rods. The roof trusses are iron and so, too, are the large plates which form the covering of the roof. Stone, brick and iron are the materials and no combustible matter is found in the construction. From the dock, the warehouses stand sublime and, from the river, their great bulk rises above the Mersey Wall. Seen from the ferry boats, this is a fitting podium for the townscape of cathedral towers. When the south docks were abandoned by commercial shipping, these warehouses became redundant and for years their fate hung in the balance. They then displayed their most impressive grandeur. The Architects' Journal called their style, cyclopean Classicism, 'a monumental masterpiece of metal and masonry construction', and the Daily Telegraph sent Don McCullin to photograph their awesome grandeur, their dark brooding shapes looming above the glucose mud which slooped moodily in the basin. This was the very epitome of the Sublime. But no buildings could continue to exist in that state however romantic it might appear to the occasional spectator. There were schemes to pull them down, others to convert them into offices, one developer proposing to fill in the dock and park cars there, and, at one time, it looked as though the Liverpool Polytechnic would be moved into them. Eventually, with the establishment of the Merseyside Development Corporation, a bold project was unveiled. With the help of government money the warehouses were converted into a tourist attraction, with offices, shops, restaurants and flats and with the establishment of the Maritime Museum and the Tate Gallery of Liverpool [220]. Although much of the sombre grandeur of the original design has disappeared and the work has been prettified, it has, at least, been saved from destruction. The conversion, carried out with great enthusiasm and care, has transformed the warehouses and an admirable new use found for old buildings.

56 **St George's Hall**

Competition 1839
St George's Plateau and Lime Street, L1
Architect: Harvey Lonsdale Elmes,
completed by Professor Charles Robert Cockerell
Engineer: Sir Robert Rawlinson. Heating Engineer: Dr David Boswell Reid

In 1839 an open competition was launched for a new concert hall to cost £30,000. In the following year, the Corporation invited competitors for the design of Assize Courts on an adjoining site. Both competitions were won by Harvey Lonsdale Elmes, an architect in his early twenties. The Corporation then decided to combine the two buildings into one major scheme and, after some deliberation, appointed Elmes for the task. This monumental undertaking occupied Elmes' lifetime but so consumed his energy that he died of consumption, a genius of English architecture burnt out at the early age of 33. The building combines the massiveness of a Roman bath with the delicacy of a Greek temple; brilliant idea of combining Roman spatial engineering with exquisite Greek detailing, and getting it all right. The plan of the interior, like the giant baths of Caracalla in Rome, is arranged on a central axis, the general idea being to create a vista 300ft (91m) long, from court to court, through the central hall. A monumental pillared front extends along Lime Street. The south front is a Greek temple portico, its tympanum once filled with lively sculpture designed by Cockerell and amended by Alfred Stevens. At the north end lies the semi-circular concert hall, its exquisite interior designed by Cockerell after Elmes' death. The building has been seen as the greatest classical monument of the 19th century. Richard Norman Shaw called it 'one of the great edifices of the world', and Richardson described its designer – 'Within the space of eight short years, the career of Elmes had flashed with meteoric brilliance across the architectural firmament, dazzling all by the intensity of its light, and on departure leaving tangible evidence of its transit'.

The building is also interesting technically, for it shows an early example of close collaboration at the design stage between the architect and the heating engineer, Dr Boswell Reid. They provided a building which solved most of the heating and ventilating problems and formed a model for later generations. Air was introduced under the long portico of the east side of the building and passed over jets of fresh water which could be regulated from a gentle shower to a saturating mist. The water cleaned the air before it entered the main rooms of the buildings. Four great shafts were incorporated in the structure, each with three compartments, two to withdraw smoke and a third for vitiated air. This fine building, one of the greatest in England and a monument of world importance, has now been extensively restored and it is possible to see the splendid Minton tile floor which forms the base of the magnificent interior. The building is fully described in Loraine Knowles' admirable monograph, *St George's Hall, Liverpool*, 1988.

57 Springwood

1839

Corner of Springwood Avenue and Woolton Road, L19

An elegant villa, it has a symmetrical ashlar facade divided into three parts by thick plain pilasters with their projecting cornices and balusters on the stone parapet which partly hides the hipped roof. It is an English country villa transported to the suburbs of Liverpool, adapted with austerity for an early Victorian mode of Neo-Classicism.

58 Liverpool Collegiate Institution

Competition 1840-43

Shaw Street, L6

Architect: Harvey Lonsdale Elmes

The Liverpool Collegiate, was founded in 1839, the first of the great Victorian public schools, to be followed by Cheltenham (1841), Marlborough (1843), Rossall (1844), Radley (1847), Lancing (1848), Bradfield (1850) and Wellington (1853). A site was chosen in Shaw Street near to the fashionable housing area of Everton which then contained some of Liverpool's finest mansions. The founders instituted an architectural competition for a building 'in the Tudor style of architecture' as being appropriate for an educational establishment. The submissions were anonymous and the first prize went to young Harvey Lonsdale Elmes, then 26 – a triple first, for he had already won competitions for St George's Hall and the Assize Courts, a quite remarkable achievement. However, it was an unhappy project, for Elmes quarrelled with his clients over fees, supervision and internal planning, so that only the facade can be said to be representative of his wishes, although even here there have been minor modifications around the entrance. The school committee was desperately short of money in the early years and tried hard to economise. The facade, for that is really all Elmes contributed, is built of Woolton red sandstone. It consists of a front of ten tall Gothic windows embracing the two main floors, and binding a centrepiece consisting of a giant Tudor arch carried the full height of the building and with its window deeply recessed behind. The roof line is crenellated and towers project at each end, containing tall oriel windows each crowned by a niche containing a carved statue. For Elmes, a man steeped in the Classical style, it is a fine achievement in the best Gothic style of educational architecture. The interior was recently gutted by fire but the fine facade seems to be intact. It is now been tastefully converted into flats.

59 **Great George Street Congregational Church**
1840-41
Great George Street, L1
Architect: Joseph Franklin

The building, affectionately known as 'The Blackie', stands on the site of an earlier chapel built between 1811 and 1812 but destroyed in a fire, when, within two hours, the whole of the interior was consumed. On the day of the fire, the congregation decided to rebuild the church and by that evening £3,672 had already been raised. The new church was designed by the Corporation architect, seated about 2,000 and cost in all £13,922, including the organ by William Hill of London, designed by Henry John Gauntlett. It is a fine Classical building consisting of a circular columnial porch, crowned by a shallow dome and attached to a rectangular meeting room of excellent acoustic quality. An oval-shaped gallery on palm leaf cast iron columns is expressed externally by two floors of windows embraced within the full-height pilasters which continue the rhythm of the portico. Reilly called it one of the best Classical buildings in the town. 'With its fine circular Corinthian portico and dome it is an elegant thing. Of course, it might be anything from a museum to a market hall, so that it does not suffer too protesting and reformed an attitude to the surrounding very agreeable decay. It is just a pleasant object, which I hope, will long remain.' It is now being used as an art and community centre.

60 Albert Public House

c1840

Lark Lane, L17

A self-confident piece of early Victorian pub architecture where, although the business of drinking was probably confined to the ground floor rooms, the brewers were prepared to build an equally elegant first floor with an oriel window hanging out over Lark Lane, and pierce the roofline with groups of stone-faced dormer windows and elaborate chimney pieces. Notice how the corner has been chamfered so that the entrance to the bar could be made on the diagonal to allow more room for the drinkers to spill out onto the pavement.

61 Fulwood Park

c1840

Off Aigburth Road, Aigburth, L17

This is the first of three private parks built in the 1840s off one of the main approach roads to Liverpool, although Rock Park across the Mersey appears to have been founded earlier, in 1836. As rich merchants moved out of the city centre to form new suburbs, this was an experiment probably unique to this city. Each park, which ran down towards the River Mersey, was laid out with great houses, mainly in the Regency style, the largest being in Fulwood Park, each with its own spacious garden planted with forest trees. Most of these large villas have had to be converted into flats. The approach to the park was barred by stately entrance gates and a park lodge. Fulwood Park consists of a single road from the gates to the small wood above the River Mersey where a locked gate keeps the park private. Originally the gardens were separated from the road by low stone walls and cast iron railings. Unfortunately, during the Second World War, the railings were removed as a misdirected patriotic gesture to build armaments, but the material proved useless. Their removal has resulted in the building of various perimeters, including concrete block walls, which has done much to reduce the attractiveness of the road. Mainly after that war some gardens were subdivided and smaller new houses built on the plots. Some have been well designed by good architects, but others are less attractive. However, the large trees maintain a silvan feeling in what is now a conservation area. The proprietors of the park insisted that the Cheshire Lines Railway ran in a tunnel under the park and thus they were denied a convenient railway station to commute into Liverpool. However, most of the houses had their own coach houses and their owners could travel by private coach into the city.

62   Grassendale Park

c1840

Entrance via Grassendale Road off the
end of Aigburth Road, L19

Slightly later than Fulwood Park, this
elegant park has two roads in it and
some of its houses face onto a
promenade on the banks of the Mersey.
There are fine decorative examples of
Regency architecture with excellent cast
iron balconies and classical details.
Some of the houses are semi-detached
and, being smaller than the large villas in
Fulwood Park, have remained in single
occupancy.

63   Cressington Park

c1840

Entrance through Salisbury Road
off St Mary's Road, L19

This is the last of the three private parks
built running down to the River Mersey
and, from an architectural point of view,
the least satisfying although there are
some charming houses in the Park. From
a lodge and park gates, two roads lead
down to a promenade.

64   Houses in Hadassah Grove

1840s

Hadassah Grove, off Lark Lane, L17

A cul-de-sac of charming little houses set in a private area screened by its own entrance gates, an idea copied from the other private parks of Liverpool, like Fulwood Park.

65   London Life Building

1841

Derby Square, L1

A tall classical facade, its symmetry only broken by placing the door to one side, bound by tall Corinthian pilasters and a very powerful broken pediment. Its proportions are whimsical, suggesting an overgrown Roman temple, but the way in which the top floor window frames are pushed into the architrave is a Mannerist detail straight from Palladio's Renaissance Palazzo del Capitanio in Vicenza.

66 Prince's Park

1842-44

Main entrance approached from Princes Avenue, L8

Architects: Sir Joseph Paxton and James Pennethorne

This was the turn of the tide that was to transform a crowded town of close-packed terrace houses into an extension to the south of Liverpool of suburbs of greenery with detached and semi-detached villas set with forest trees and with open public parkland on a scale unknown in other English cities. Prince's Park was the brain child of Richard Vaughan Yates who purchased some 90 acres from Lord Sefton with the idea of creating a park with trees and a lake open to the public, surrounded by private villas whose construction would pay for the cost of the park. Picton, in praise, wrote 'all honour to the man whose benevolence devised and whose perseverance carried out the scheme'. It was to be a place where 'bright green lawns sparkle in the sun, and within the same distance from a crowded town it would be difficult to find a pleasanter locality'. Designed a year earlier than the more sophisticated Birkenhead Park, this was Paxton's first commission outside Chatsworth. It is obviously much influenced by Nash's Regent's Park which was begun in 1809 but carries further the concept of a picturesque park layout surrounded by suburban housing, for here the terraces and detached villas are arranged informally around the perimeter. It is a major architectural statement with the landscape carefully formed and composed to create a beautiful picture. The style derives from the informal layouts by Lancelot (Capability) Brown (1715-1783) who was the designer of many of the fine private landscape parks of 18th century England. From his designs the ideas spread to France and the flowing curves of paths and lakes became a feature of the Paris parks. Paxton brought the theme to Merseyside at this park and at Birkenhead Park. Paths were designed for leisurely perambulation so that they traversed the maximum distance on a very limited area. Views were composed as a painter would compose a landscape painting and the total effect was largely aesthetic. Although the cost of the park layout was defrayed by the sale of building plots and was eventually a commercial success, to begin with the park was the private domain of those who lived in the houses, rather as the gardens of the London squares and those of Falkner and Abercromby Squares in Liverpool were reserved for the exclusive use of the house owners. Only later was Prince's Park thrown open to the general public although the idea was there from the start. Thus the concept was quite different from Birkenhead Park which, from its inception, was designed for public use. Some of the houses around Prince's Park were indeed stately with classical facades of great elegance. From the fine cast iron main gates of the park, reputed to have been designed by Decimus Burton (1800-1881) who, in 1825, laid out Hyde Park in London, a tree-lined Princes Avenue heads towards the city centre. It has long been rumoured that Decimus Burton also had a hand in the design of some of the classical houses. He was an architect of some repute who travelled at great speed all over the country. At 23 he had designed the dome of the Colosseum in London's Hyde Park, a sort of Greek Pantheon with its dome larger than that of St Paul's. Colvin says 'he was neither a scholar nor an archaeologist, and although he travelled in Greece and Italy in later life, he relied for his detail on the published works of others rather than on personal investigation'. He must have known Yates for, in 1827, he designed a house for his brother, Joseph Brooks Yates, at West Dingle not far from the site of the park. When the park was being built he was engaged by Sir Peter Fleetwood-Hesketh to design the new town of Fleetwood on the Lancashire coast and then, in 1843, he went to do some work in Cork, probably travelling via Liverpool.

67   Watchmen's huts, Canning Half-tide Dock

1844

South Docks, L1

Architect: Jesse Hartley

These are lovely tailor-made gate houses in which the men who opened and closed the lock gates could take shelter and rest. Jesse Hartley at his best; one feels he must have enjoyed designing them. Each is individually styled and constructed with meticulous care of Scottish granite, every piece fitting precisely into place like some large jig-saw puzzle and the roof capped in tooled solid granite, topped by a playful stone pinnacle.

68   Victoria Tower

1845-48

Salisbury Dock in the Northern Dock System and opposite Stanley Dock, Regent Road, L3

Architect: Jesse Hartley

For Picton, 'Jesse Hartley was a man of genius, of sterling integrity, and stern independence and self-reliance'. Unlike his other dock towers built to house hydraulic machinery, this is simply a clock and bell tower modelled on the castle architecture of the Rhine, but unmistakably the work of Jesse Hartley. Rather gauche, it stands solidly, built of the same grey granite blocks as his warehouses, carefully dressed and fitted together like an intricate jig-saw puzzle. The upper part is hexagonal with a unique six-faced clock and a high placed bell to ring out the high tide and warning notes. Masonry crisp, clear and finely assembled rises from a circular stone base. It was built to commemorate the opening of Salisbury Dock. Let us hope that Alexander Gage's remarks of 1841 are heeded, 'Mr Hartley's works are intended for posterity'.

69 **Branch Bank of England**
1845-48
Castle Street, L1
Architect: Professor Charles Robert Cockerell

A gem of Castle Street and probably Cockerell's masterpiece. It is a building, according to Reilly, 'which alone would give character and quality to the street. Although no larger than its neighbours, it is bigger in scale – that is to say, bigger and stronger in its parts – than any building in Liverpool, save St George's Hall, and like St George's Hall it combines strength with refinements, as all good works should do'. Its main facade consists of a free adaptation of pure Greek detail used in a way that no 5th century Greek architect would have adopted, probably because he would never have thought of it. Cockerell's Bank House, which once stood to the rear in Cook Street, has been demolished. Another sad loss for it was a pioneer work in the development of office buildings where the fenestration had to be enlarged to allow adequate daylight to enter the offices.

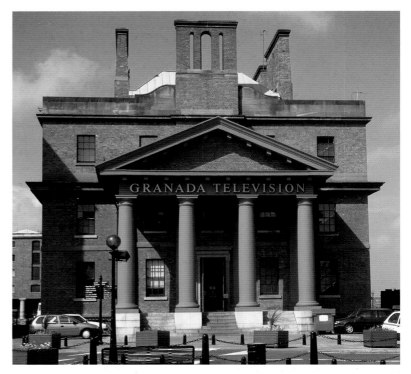

71   Albert Dock Traffic Office
1846-47
South Docks, L1
Architect: Phillip Hardwick with the top storey added by Jesse Hartley

The supreme architectural achievement of Victorian self-confidence. Tucked into the north-eastern corner of the Albert Dock Warehouses, it is a splendid cast iron building by Phillip Hardwick of Euston Arch fame. Its facade consists of a Tuscan columnial portico, in scale and grandeur reminiscent of his ill-fated London arch. The fascination lies in the fact that the whole of the portico is cast in iron. The columns are shafts of iron, 17ft 8in (5·4m) high, cast in two halves and brazed together along their length – each has a diameter of 3ft 2in (94cm) at the base. As far as can be seen the architrave is more remarkable, consisting of a single casting which is 36ft (11m) long shaped in the form of a giant U beam 2ft 7in (76cm) square. Brazed on to this architrave is an iron cornice and frieze consisting of seven separate castings. Where else in the world can one find such a monument to cast iron architecture, that great building material of the Victorians? It has now been taken over and used by Granada Television.

70   Roman Catholic Church of St Francis Xavier
1845-49
Salisbury Street, L3
Architect: J J Scoles

An impressive stone church in the transitional Gothic style between Early English and Decorated with mainly Decorated tracery. It has a tall tower and spire placed in the corner adjacent to the west end and forming the entrance porch. The aisled interior has tall slender marble columns. Built almost as a separate building in 1888, Edmund Kirby's flamboyant Lady Chapel is a splendid adjunct at the south-east corner.

72   Sailors' Home

1846-52, burnt 1860 and rebuilt 1862, now demolished

Canning Place, L1

Architect: John Cunningham

Another sad casualty to demolition and quite unnecessarily pulled down, John
Cunningham's seaman's lodging house was modelled on such Elizabethan mansions
as Woolaton and Hardwick Hall. A vivacious carved portal once led straight into the
magnificent glazed courtyard where tier upon tier of cast iron balconies narrowed in
'V' formation. As a monument it was superb, a sort of small scaled Milan Galleria, but
one can understand that its forbidding interior lacked the homely attractiveness
demanded by the modern sailor home on leave. Surely an alternate use could have
been found for it. The cast iron gates were preserved and have gone to a Midlands'
museum and some of the panels, decorated with a mermaid, were taken by Clough
Williams-Ellis for Portmerion. One now faces one of the county offices in the old town
at Caernarvon, having been placed there by the architect, Dewi Prys-Thomas, a
Liverpool lecturer who was largely responsible for their preservation.

73   Allerton Tower Lodge

1847

Woolton Road, Woolton, L18

Architect: Harvey Lonsdale Elmes

Allerton Tower was one of a group of stately homes laid out in landscaped parks some
five miles south of the city centre. Each was designed for a wealthy merchant to display
the power and affluence of the 19th century entrepreneurs of Liverpool and the work
was carried out by notable national architects. Elmes, when attempting anything but a
great classical design, was decidedly disappointing. Druids Cross, an Italianate villa,
was an anticlimax after his brilliant work on St George's Hall and has now been
demolished to make way for a suburban housing estate. Only the rather dull stable
block remains This is the place to mention the sad fate of this once splendid group of
country houses. Allerton Park was designed in 1815 by Thomas Harrison of Chester,
the architect of the Lyceum. Built for the merchant, Jacob Fletcher, it was destroyed by
fire. Part of the ground floor remains, incorporated into a golf club house, a sad
reminder of its former quality. Only the original lodge is now intact. Allerton Towers,
built in 1847 also by Elmes, was disappointing but the small lodge on Woolton Road,
here illustrated, is attractive with its circular domed peristyle temple forming a porch
attached to a small single storey Victorian house. The orangery is also by Elmes.
Cleveleys, designed for the cotton merchant, Sir Joseph Leather, by Sir George Gilbert
Scott in 1865 is now demolished. All that remains is a lodge and a stable block.
Allerton Priory [109], of 1867-70, designed by Alfred Waterhouse for Grant-Morris, a
colliery owner, is still there and is described further on. Harthill, built for the shipping
magnate, John Bibby, has gone and only the gates remain as an entrance to
Calderstones Park [98]. Allerton Beeches, designed by Richard Norman Shaw for the
Tate family in 1884, has been destroyed. And finally, his Mere Bank, which had been
designed for HD Horsfall in 1886 and which once stood in Ullet Road, was
demolished as late as 1964. The architectural taste of the Liverpool merchant princes
seems to have swung between two extremes of the austere and the flamboyant with
little in between. This splendid heritage of irreplaceable mansions has, in many cases,
been wantonly thrown away.

74   Walton Gaol

c1848-55

Hornby Road, Walton, L9

Architect: John Weightman, Corporation Surveyor

Portentous castellated Norman best seen from the outside. One inmate was heard to remark 'stone walls and iron bars do not a prison make – but they sure help'. By the use of symbolism the architect has tried to suggest the strength implied in military architecture and this has now been carried a stage further for the original castle facade has largely been obscured by an impressive brick bastion which runs the full length of the front, topped with a large metal cavetto string course to keep the prisoners in. Only the upper stages of the original towers peep out over the long horizontal band of brickwork.

75   Hydraulic Tower

c1848

Stanley Dock, Regents Road, L3

Architect: Jesse Hartley

A miniature medieval castle designed by Jesse Hartley to pump water pressure for the opening of locks and swing bridges, one of a group to be found throughout his dockland. Each is individually designed and each uses the symbolism of military architecture, with machicolation from which boiling oil could be thrown on attackers, narrow arrow slits for defensive artillery and crenellation on the skyline. It is part of Hartley's attempt to suggest strength and inviolability which has further expression in the massive wall and gate posts he built to seal off the docks from the Dock Road. The pump house is built beside the tall octagonal tower which, itself, partly conceals the round chimney. Real picturesque industrial architecture; he must have persuaded his clients to pay for the extra embellishments.

76 School for the Blind

1850
Now Police Headquarters
Hardman Street, L1
Architect: AH Holme

Liverpool built the first school for the indigent blind in the country. This was largely the inspiration of of a Liverpool merchant, Edward Rushton, who had been stricken blind when accompanying slaves on a slave ship to the West Indies. As a result, he became an ardent anti-slave activist and instigated the building of the first Blind School in Commutation Row in 1790. This, the second school, has a long low classical facade with a central bay and wings giving it a Hellenistic look. It is a fairly late example of Liverpool Greek Revival but with a strange arrangement of the wings where paired windows on two storeys have been inserted in columnar porticoes, requiring a central Ionic column, an unusual feature of a central solid not often found in Greece, but occasionally in the early Italian Renaissance. Fra Giocondo did it at Verona and Leonardo da Vinci in one of his sketches. Tacked on to one end there is an elegant two-storey ashlar addition dating from the 1930s which fits in well. The building is now partly used as a police station and as the Merseyside Trades Union Community and Unemployed Resource Centre. The 1930s extension, admirably carried out on the corner of Hardman Street and Hope Street, replaced John Foster Junior's Chapel for the School, designed as a Greek Temple, a form so beloved to Foster with his archaeological background. The new building reflects the return to Classicism which characterised the work of architects influenced by Charles Reilly and the British School at Rome where Anthony Minoprio had been a Rome Scholar. Its emphasis on Classical form and proportion and its thin Greek detailing was also inspired by architecture in America and by some of the of the buildings of the Fascist regime in Italy. James Woodford, another Rome scholar, designed the noble bronze doors which once opened from Hardman Street and Hope Street but which have now been transferred to the School in Wavertree. Inspired by church doors he had seen in Italy, such as those at St Zeno at Verona, Woodford produced these large plain bronze panels each with its three sculptured reliefs of crafts worked on by the blind. Woodford's work can also be seen on the doors of the RIBA in Portland Place, London, and on Norwich City Hall, another building designed by a Liverpool graduate and a Rome scholar.

77 Mornington Terrace

Mid-19th century
Duke Street, L1

A fine late Georgian terrace of five houses, each of three floors, unified by a central pediment and gilded nameplate. Each house is subordinated to the overall design of the terrace and the whole composition is carefully and beautifully proportioned. Many of the houses have now been converted into offices.

78 Windermere Terrace

Mid-19th century

Windermere Terrace, L8

A particularly fine group of three-storey terraces and a villa backing onto Prince's Park and forming a crescent of Regency-style buildings. The elegance of the facades and the sylvan setting running into the greenery of the park have made them delightful retreats so close to the centre of a great city. This is a rare example of the back elevations, facing onto the park, being even finer than the fronts. They form a unified composition with a flat centrepiece, canopied balconies with graceful coupled iron columns and projecting bays rising to the full height of the terrace.

79 Houses in Upper Parliament Street

Mid-19th century

Upper Parliament Street, L8

On the outer edge of an extensive Georgian area, it has many fine Georgian-style houses. Some of the finest were at the lower end of the street and have been demolished, but there are still good examples facing the east end of the Anglican Cathedral. A gap, adjacent to Percy Street, has been filled with a modern block built in sympathy with its neighbours [223]. The most successful remaining terrace in Regency stucco runs between Grove Street and Sandon Street and was completely reconstructed after the damage of the Toxteth riots which had burned down the Racquet Club on the other side of the road.

80 Norwich Union Building

c1850

Castle Street, L1

This is one of numerous Victorian buildings in the street, a representative classical facade of considerable dignity and a valuable neighbour to the Bank of England. It consists of a ground floor of windows and a door, bounded by pilasters and a cornice which stand upon a broad plinth. This forms the solid base for a classical Corinthian temple front which overlays the windows of the two upper floors. What a strange solution to an office building, yet it is eminently successful for it emphasises the individual character of the building and, at the same time, seems to link it to its neighbours.

81 National Provincial Bank

c1850

Water Street, L1

A well-proportioned Italian Renaissance building in the style of the Italian Renaissance architect, Sanmicheli. It might be Verona, but it is in the middle of a northern commercial city. Notice how the edges are sharply defined by pilasters and a columnial screen of Renaissance Doric columns is inserted between them, the outer columns close spaced to pair with their adjoining pilasters. These all stand like some Italian palazzo on a rusticated base, originally intended to emphasise the importance of the first floor, the piano nobile, but here a little inappropriate for the main banking hall was on the ground floor. At least the Victorians carried out their impersonations with panache! The front is excellent, but the side looks awkwardly tacked on.

82 **Midland Railway Goods Station**

c1850, completed 1874, and 1995-96

Now the Conservation Centre for the National Museums and Galleries on Merseyside

Victoria Street, Crosshall Street and Whitechapel, L1

Architect for the conversion: Ken Martin

Professor Reilly called this one of the best buildings in the town. 'The purposes for which a goods station exists are, I suppose, to receive, store and forward merchandise. Great gateways, therefore, are essential, and high plain walls. There is obviously an opportunity here for dignity and the Midland Railway has seized it. The main front has a slightly concave face which seems to suggest a readiness for reception. The cliff-like wall, in a good dark brick, is articulated with a row of fine arched windows, and is crowned with a strong stone quoin. The two great doorways, big enough to receive the most piled up lorry, are placed symmetrically towards the end of the facade, and are of great strong shape. It is altogether a very strong and pleasant piece of good building, proving again that architecture is not a matter of features but of proportion and expression.' Taking advantage of the existing features and preserving the exterior, the building has now been largely rebuilt inside in an imaginative manner to provide conservation workshops for the National Galleries and Museums on Merseyside. The utilitarian character of the old building has been maintained in the large, bold spaces provided inside so that all manner of large objects can be brought in and easily moved about so that they can be worked on and preserved. The bold, factory-like character of the building has been maintained, but imaginative, three-dimensional spaces have been inserted, high lit by bold sculpture, so that the building can be used by the public as a recreative and instructional centre. The architect of the conservation project is Ken Martin, previously head of the Polytechnic School of Architecture, now the Centre for Architecture of the John Moores University.

83 Wapping Dock Warehouse
c1850, opened 1856
South Docks, L1
Architect: Jesse Hartley

In 1846 Jesse Hartley, Dock Surveyor from 1824 to his death in 1860, prepared a scheme to provide additional accommodation by enlarging Salthouse Dock eastwards with the construction of a new basin called Wapping Dock. This was to bypass the Duke of Bridgewater's system, with its intrusive canal running at right angles to the line of the docks, which had become a barrier to expansion. The warehouse, which is modelled in style on the Albert Dock Warehouses [55], is 760ft long, 75ft 6in wide and 58ft high, (232 x 23 x 18m) designed throughout on a noble scale. The construction is fireproof and the building designed in five fireproof sections. Hydraulic lifts provided communication between floors. It has a row of cast iron Doric columns supporting occasional elliptical arches of two storey height along the edge of the basin. But it is the fine red brickwork, carefully spaced windows and modest brick cornice which give the design of this warehouse its essential character of engineering architecture of a very high order. The building has now been converted into luxury flats, some with fine views over the dock and the River Mersey.

84 Stanley Dock Warehouse
1852-56
North Docks, Regents Road, L3
Architect: Jesse Hartley

An extension of the enclosed system used at the Albert Dock Warehouses [55]. Two warehouse blocks faced each other across the Stanley Dock which was opened in 1848. However, in 1897 part of the dock was filled in to provide a site for the large Tobacco Bonded Warehouse [157] which was opened in 1900, obscuring one of the blocks from view in the dock. The buildings are similar to those at Wapping Dock. Their cast iron columns are a modified version of those used on the Albert Dock Warehouses. They are a more logical design for hollow drums and curve inwards, in profile, in contrast to the Greek entasis used on their cast iron prototypes on the Albert Dock.

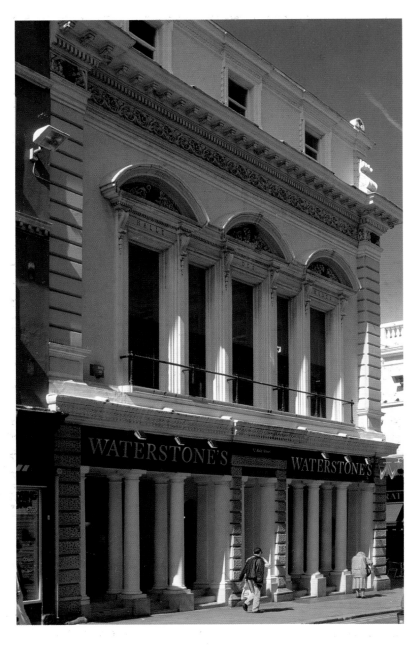

85   Marlborough House
1853
Now Waterstones Bookshop
52 Bold Street, L1
Architect: AH Holme

An earlier Victorian building has been remodelled with a rusticated base containing
shop windows and a richly carved frieze above, to become a concert hall. Although
no longer used for that purpose, it is still a fine powerful building.

86   Church of St Mary the Virgin
1853-56
Almonds Green, West Derby Village, L12
Architect: Sir George Gilbert Scott

Superbly sited alongside the entrance gates to Croxteth Hall [6] and in the centre of
what was once West Derby village, this is a Victorian church in the grand style. Big in
scale as one might expect from the work of Gilbert Scott. Built in Scott's beloved
Decorated Gothic style, it consists of a Latin Cross plan with a tall proud tower over the
crossing. It has tall transepts and a polygonal apse. Inside, height and sombre red
sandstone create a feeling of dignity and nobility, just what Lord Sefton, who
commissioned this estate church, would have wished.

87 Everton Waterworks

1854-57

Aubrey Street, L6

Architect: Thomas Duncan, the Corporation's first water engineer

A one and a half acre service reservoir 12ft (3·6m) deep was constructed in 1854, but the most impressive visual feature is the high level tank, a circular structure supported on stone arches and brick and masonry cross arches which radiate from a central column. The tank is cast in iron and holds 2,700 gallons at 90ft (27m) above the pavement. Powerful Victorian engineering at its most impressive; its scale is massive and reminds one of the heroic remains of ancient Rome depicted in the etchings of Piranesi.

88 Liverpool & London & Globe Building

1855-57

Dale Street, L1

Architects: Professor.CR Cockerell and FP Cockerell

A fine stone building on the right of the Town Hall by the architect of the Branch Bank of England. 'It is strong and powerful, and has the only originality worth the name in architecture, that which comes from the reflection of strong personality combined with great knowledge', wrote Reilly. It contained many features dear to the Cockerells, father and son, such as the shape of the ground floor windows and the iron balconies on the second floor. The main door is unusual in the way in which a pedimented portal is inserted with a festooned stone frame which climbs above the first floor windows as though once designed for a larger building. The diagonal lines of the staircases are cleverly expressed on the side facade, a most unclassical feature. The original proportions of this building are marred by the later addition of a mansard roof containing dormer windows.

89   Albany

1856-58

Old Hall Street, L1

Architect: JK Colling

This is one of the best of the large Victorian office blocks. It successfully
combines company offices with warehouse accommodation. The facade is
brick and stone, allowing Colling, an erudite London architect with a
passion for foliated ornament, to exercise his affection on the intricate incised
carved detailing over the doors and windows. Steps lead to a raised
entrance lobby, then drop to the impressive whitewashed courtyard which
occupies the centre of the building. This is spanned at first floor level by a
lace-like cast iron bridge reached by a spiral stair. Were it not reminiscent of
an American penitentiary, the court would seem most attractive, and it
certainly provides good lighting in adjoining rooms. The plan is ingenious,
for in addition to a large central court, there are two long top-glazed
galleries down each side of the building which provide additional day
lighting.

90   Roman Catholic Church of St Vincent de Paul

1856-57

St James Street, L1

Architect: EW Pugin

This is one of the many comparatively simple Roman Catholic churches built in the
dockyard areas to serve the influx of Irish labour in the 1840s. St Vincent de Paul
exemplified compassion for the poor, orphans and prisoners. The church was designed
by ANW Pugin's son and the exterior is characterised by a playful light lantern on the
apex of the roof.

91 **Magistrates Courts**
   1857-59
   Dale Street,
   opposite Crosshall Street, L1
   Architect: John Weightman

A symmetrical plain but well-proportioned three-storey facade in ashlar with a large central carriage entrance spanned by a segmental arch through which the magistrates could make their leisurely way to the courts. Stylistically it looks rather earlier.

92 **Hargreaves Building**
   Completed 1859
   Chapel Street, L1
   Architect: James Picton

Sir James Picton (1805-89) was the notable Liverpool architect who originated the public library and museum. His best building, Richmond House, has now been demolished but this is another fine example of his robust handling of a commercial premises. It was built for the Liverpool merchant, Sir William Brown, on three storeys in the Venetian palazzo style with, on the ground floor, round-headed windows, each containing a large semi-circular headed central pane of glass supported on decorated cast iron mullions. Above the windows there are carved plaques in the style of Brunelleschi depicting famous people involved in the exploration of the New World: Anacona, Amerigo, Bermeja, Ferdinand, Columbus, Isabella, Cortez and Pizarrro.

93　11 Dale Street

1859

Dale Street, L1

Architect: James Picton

Originally the Union Marine Buildings, it was designed by Sir James Allanson Picton (1805-89), author of *The Memorials of Liverpool* which is such a mine of information on the early architecture of the city, and an architect with strong views. This is typical of his work, a powerful round arched building with a rusticated semi-basement. In Florentine style, the building is capped with a very heavy projecting cornice, but here, to symbolise the maritime tradition of Liverpool, consisting of a rope moulding on round-arched machicolations.

94　The Liverpool Museum and Library

1859-60

William Brown Street, L1

Architects: Thomas Allom and John Weightman

The first of the range of Classical buildings running down the hill and adjoining the north end of St George's Hall. The main front is a Corinthian-styled Roman temple approached by a monumental flight of steps. It is a splendid example of the way in which the civic pride of a great 19th century commercial city in England could import a Roman example of architecture to enhance its visual impact.

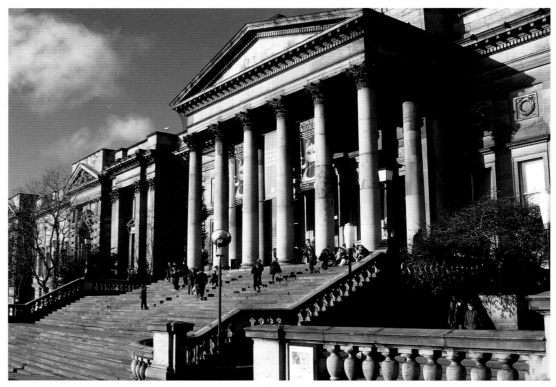

95 Export Carriage and Wheelworks

1859, now destroyed

28 St Anne's Street, L3

Sadly, now destroyed by fire, a cast iron facade reminiscent of the southern States of America and of work in Glasgow. Picton described it as 'among the very handsome buildings which Liverpool contains. This must be considered one of the ornaments of the town. The interior is arranged at the front of the building with large, commodious and very light showrooms, wherein are on view very handsome and first class carriages of every description. In architecture, properly so called, iron is destined to play a very important part. Hitherto architects as a body have neglected iron. Well employed, they have striven to hide it from sight and then seemed to apologise to themselves and the world for being obliged to use it instead of brick or stone. Its use, however, is being forced upon us and on every side we are confronted with iron sheds, iron churches, iron houses. The designs of these are usually hideous to behold, and why should this be so? Why should architects not face the difficulty, and instead of letting iron master them, convert it to their handmaiden and servant?' Picton was thus able to use this building as an example to support his aim to bring 19th century architecture up to date in a conservative atmosphere.

96 Old Municipal Buildings

1860-66

Dale Street, L1

Architect: begun by John Weightman, Corporation Surveyor, completed by his successor, ER Robson

A large block containing an amalgam of French, Classical and Gothic Revival detail. Of it, Reilly wrote, 'The lower part of the tower is very fine; the spire is merely humorous. It has a wrought iron balcony half way down, like a skirt popped over the head (if that is ever done) and not allowed to settle into its proper place'. The property at the back was destroyed in the Second World War leaving a dull brick back elevation and a car park which should be built upon to complete the street and hide this back.

97 Cressington Park Station

Opened 1861

Knowsley Road, Cressington Park, L19

A lovely little Victorian railway station on what was originally the Cheshire Lines Railway. Opened in 1861, it carried passengers on a charming green route to and from the city centre in the underground station at Central. The station buildings are more picturesque than beautiful, with a piled-up Victorian block containing the administration on one side and pretty lace-frilled canopies on ornamental iron, projecting to give limited protection from the weather over part of the two platforms.

98 Calderstones Park Entrance Gates

1861-63

The corner of Calderstones Road and Harthill Road, L18

Architect: James Picton

Originally this was the entrance to John Bibby's mansion at Harthill, but they now form the approach to a fine Liverpool park. The centrepiece consists of two massive ashlar piers with, standing in front on a reversed console, two gigantic Atlantes, their arms stretched up to their heads to support impost blocks and cornice. Atlantes were first mentioned by the Roman writer, Vitruvius, and were sometimes used instead of columns to support an entablature. The word probably comes from Atlas, one of the Titans who was punished by Zeus and made to support the heavens with his head and hands. They are similar to caryatids and Persians, except that these portrayed women and prisoners of war in bondage, captured by the victorious Greeks. These powerful Liverpool statues were taken from Brown's Building, an office block designed by JA Picton in 1861 where they originally stood. A wall continues on each side of the gateway, decorated with four more statues representing the Seasons, an appropriate entrance to a park.

99   Anfield Cemetery
1862
Entrance at the corner of Priory Road and Walton Lane, L4
Architects: Lucy & Littler

What a wonderful age that can demonstrate its affluence with such exuberance in architecture! Three elaborate iron gates with stone piers and a central pinnacle rising high into the air and ornately carved with the crest of the city, proclaim the monumental entrance to this cemetery. A fitting announcement for the final journey! At one side stands a Gothic lodge, its entrance dated 1872.

100 Wellington Column
1863
William Brown Street and Lime Street, L1
Architect: Lawson of Glasgow

The noble figure of Wellington is perched precariously on a lofty fluted Doric column. This, and the Steble Fountain of the late 1870s, its cast iron figures sunbathing at the base, fill in the space of the Victorian roundabout at the point of junction between the axis of St George's Hall and the civic buildings in William Brown Street. The standard measures at 62 degrees Fahrenheit verified by the Standards Department of the Board of Trade, are sculptured on a bronze panel attached to the base of the column. With the change to metric, this will become something of a museum piece.

101 Oriel Chambers

1864

Water Street, L1

Architect: Peter Ellis

This is the most significant office building in Liverpool and one of the most important buildings in the world because, both stylistically and structurally, it foreshadows by many years the work of the Modern Movement in architecture. The main facades break from the traditional small-windowed Italian Renaissance design, and the oriel windows provide an adequate flood of light in the offices behind. The courtyard elevations are years in advance of their date. Long bands of plain undecorated windows are cantilevered 2ft 6in (76cm) out from the H staunchion frame which lies between the stone cross walls of the building. This facade is thus a very early example of cantilevered cladding design. Reilly described its main facades as a 'sort of honeycomb of numberless plate glass oriel windows held together by a stonework skeleton frame designed to look like cast iron. Its humour as a cellular habitation for the human insect is a distinct asset to its town'. Perhaps today we see more the significance of the design. Its predominance of glass areas and the thin lineal quality of its frame strike a most appealing note. Its windows throw back the reflections of adjoining buildings.

102 16 Cook Street Office Building

c1864, completed 1866
16 Cook Street, L1
Architect: Peter Ellis

Peter Ellis' second essay in office design, and probably his last in view of the unfavourable comments his architecture promoted. We have no evidence of further work. The facade, in spite of its large areas of glass, is less exciting than Oriel Chambers. Its triple arched frame and flowing pediment seem to foreshadow Art Nouveau, but the back elevation, which is hard to see, utilises a freedom of composition later to be exploited by Richard Norman Shaw and culminating in the work of Charles Rennie Mackintosh in Glasgow. But once again it is the courtyard that is most significant. The side elevation follows Oriel Chambers, but tucked into the corner there is an outrageously modern glazed cast iron staircase. The metal panels were inserted after the last war; replacing earlier timber panels, but the form of the glazing is original. The spiral staircase itself has no central support and appears to be cantilevered from each floor level. When he was a boy, John Wellborn Root (1850-91) was sent to Liverpool to avoid the hardships of the American Civil War and he came to Liverpool when this building was being put up. Its design was to effect this brilliant American architect who, when he built some of the fine early skyscrapers in Chicago, incorporated Ellis's ideas. For example, in the Rookery, which he designed with his partner, Daniel Burnham, in 1885, he incorporated a glass and iron spiral staircase projecting from the building somewhat similar to the one on 16 Cook Street; another example of the close cultural links that existed between Liverpool and the United States.

103 Temple

1864-65

Dale Street, L1

Architects: James Picton & Son

This occupies the whole block between Princes
Street and Temple Street on the south side of Dale
Street. It is a handsome office block with a granite
base and a stone superstructure of seven bays with
a curved bay on the corner of Princes Street. It
has a mansard roof in the French style, and a
tower for effect. This is chamfered with recessed
corners and narrows to an octagon at the upper
stage, topped by a cupola with finials. It shows the
extent to which architects could go in order to
persuade their clients that powerful statement was
directly related to additional height. See the Vines
Public House [168], an attitude of mind that was
to contribute to the erection with wild exuberance
of some of the New York skyscrapers.

104 48 Castle Street

1864

Castle Street, L1

Architect: James Picton

This is typical of Picton's office style though less robust than some of his designs. It is a strongly articulated facade of round arched openings with, between them on the ground floor and the basement, five granite columns on pedestals. The first floor has four round openings with rope mouldings and relief busts in the tympana and, above all, the usual Picton powerful cornice.

106 Presbyterian Church of Wales

1865

Now taken by another sect

Princes Road, L8

Architects: W & G Audsley

A fine example of the full-blooded Gothic in the Decorated Revival style, with the usual pronounced individuality of the work of the Audsleys. Its spiky silhouette is a feature in the street, an area once full of splendid churches. The interior is particularly impressive with all the detailing carefully thought out. Light fittings, etc. are all part of the architects' brief. Now, sadly, it has been vacated by the Welsh who have sold it to another sect. The new owners seem either incapable or unwilling to maintain this church. It is rapidly falling apart with slates off the roof and forest trees starting to sprout from the base of the tall steeple. If action is not taken it will not stand for many years more.

106 Greek Orthodox Church of St Nikolaos

1865-70

Princes Road, L8

Architect: Henry Sumners

Pink domed Byzantine splendour in the midst of Liverpool 8, its foreground setting cheapened by a rather inappropriately-sited little drive-in bank. The church is a remarkably convincing interpretation of Byzantine architecture by an architect who, elsewhere, was inclined to indulge in rogue whimsies. See, for example, his church of St Cyprian, Edge Hill [128]. Sumners was certainly a man of parts. 'The church is of brick with white stone dressings, and courses of stone introduced, alternating with the brick.' Picton goes on, 'The interior, though not so magnificent as St Isaac's at St Petersburg, nor so grand as St Sophia at Constantinople, is nevertheless handsome and well designed, but the style is not one to attract the Western nations to follow in its wake. In cases of this kind association is everything'. Fortunately there is still a lively Greek population in Liverpool to sustain the place.

107 Waterloo Grain Warehouses

1867

Waterloo Dock in the Northern System, Waterloo Road, L3

Engineer: George Fosbery Lyster

Lyster was the City Engineer, a man of many interests. For example, he designed, but fortunately never built, a floating fort to be armed with 110-ton muzzle loading guns, to guard the approaches to the River Mersey. This warehouse is an extension of the Albert Dock enclosed warehouse system, built round three sides of the dock, the end block being destroyed in the Second World War. Of these buildings, Picton wrote, 'The design is a great improvement on the massive ugliness of the Albert Warehouses. The ground floor is an open arcade supported by granite piers and arches with five vaulted floors above. The openings in each storey are double lights, with semi circular heads in brick, and rough stone string courses. The building is surrounded by a bold cornice partly corbelled out in brick with stone brackets or cantilevers. The hoisting machinery is fixed in turrets arising above the general line of the structure. On the whole, the design, though simple, is characteristic and effective, showing evidence of thought and power of adaptability'. Although today we would disagree with Picton's assessment of the Albert Dock Warehouses, his other comments are still valid. These warehouses have now been converted into luxury flats by Barratts.

108 Lime Street Station

1867-68

Lime Street, L1

Engineers: William Baker and CR Stevenson as Chief Engineer to the London and North Western Railway

In a mere 40 years three stations were constructed on this site. The first, designed by John Cunningham for the Liverpool and Manchester Railway Company, which had opened as far as Edge Hill in 1830, was completed on this site in 1836. A two-storey masonry screen on to Lime Street was added by John Foster between 1835 and 1836 to beautify the front. The second station, which was completed in 1851, was designed by Richard Turner with William Fairburn as consultant for the London and North

Western Railway. William Tite was the architect for the adjoining office buildings. In its time, this was the largest engine shed in the world, measuring 153ft 6in by 370ft long (47·7 x 112·7m). It was also the first shed in which iron had been used throughout. The third station, which was completed in 1879, cost half a million pounds. Five years earlier it had been decided to double the area by adding another arched shed with a span of 200ft (70m). Once underway, the erection of this dry form of construction was remarkably speedy and one bay only took three days to complete. It is now one of the best monuments to the great railway age. Its translucent arches and the slight curve in its length heighten its impact only slightly diminished by the modern structures erected at the end of the platforms which, from the entrance foyer, partly obscure the view of these magnificent vaults.

109 Allerton Priory and Lodge

1867-70

Allerton Road, just beyond the junction with
Heath Road, L18

Architect: Alfred Waterhouse

Good domestic Waterhouse architecture in simple
Gothic style. It is a hard-edged building in dark
brick with smoke-stained sandstone dressings, of
interest mainly to devotees of this man's work
which is so fully represented in his birthplace,
Liverpool. Waterhouse was always better when he
was working in a glazed brick, for here his brown
brickwork laced with blue bands and stone
dressings is depressing. The garden front is
symmetrical Gothic, but the general impression of
the building is of an irregular picturesque pile with
the usual Waterhouse entrance beneath a tower
and truncated spire and a silhouette of pinnacles
and spikes. It was originally a country house for a
rich colliery owner, John Grant Morris (1811-
1896), who invited Alfred Waterhouse to build
him two other residences – Crimpleshawe Hall in
Norfolk and the Villa Allerton near Cannes in the
South of France. Such was the value of coal! In its
life, Allerton Priory has been converted into a
school and, later, into an old peoples' home with
the result that unsightly steel firescapes now project
from the side elevation.

110 Sefton Park

1867-72

From Ullet Road to Aigburth Vale and the start of Queen's Drive, the park is encircled by
Aigburth Drive and Mossley Hill Drive, L17

Architects: Edouard André and Louis Hornblower

Liverpool is famous for its parks. Few cities in the western world can compare with the
green swathes of South Liverpool where parks have been laid out almost linking each
other and where splendid tree-lined avenues radiate from the city centre. Many of these
were originally landscaped as dual carriageways to allow trams to travel safely in the
central reservation, but now these trams have gone and the arboreal effect is
magnificent. South Liverpool must be one of the loveliest places in any European city.
Everywhere there are mature forest trees and open spaces on a scale unseen
elsewhere, but slowly suburban growth is eating at the edges, destroying irreplaceable
settings. At Sefton Park, the grandest of all the parks, some 400 acres were the subject
of a competition won by André of Paris, a pupil of Alphand, the great landscape
gardener of Napoleon III, and Louis Hornblower, a Liverpool architect. The influence of
the Paris parks can be seen in the use of circles and ellipse in the layout of the drives.
The scheme comprised streams and a lake, ornamental buildings, such as the Palm
House [144], a splendid iron bridge which carries the roadway over the ravine and a
peripheral arrangement of detached and semi-detached Victorian villas. The sale of the
fine sites for the villas partly defrayed the immense cost of laying out the parkland. The
lodges by Hornblower particularly merit mention. There are two; Sefton Park Lodge and
Fulwood Lodge, both built about 1870 in an elaborate Tudor half-timbered style on a
base of brick and stone, very romantic and covered with rich carvings and statuettes.
The gates to the park are also fine. Those opening to Aigburth Road have six red
granite pillars surmounted by lanterns. The centrepiece is arched and carries the City's
coat of arms.

111 Newsham Park

1868

Newsham Park, off West Derby Road, L6

Birkenhead was the first town in Britain to create a public park
when, in 1843, Joseph Paxton was called in to design the
layout. Prince's Park, Liverpool was begun by him in the same
year, but that was, initially, a private park. The first of the public
parks to be conceived for Liverpool was Newsham Park. In
1846 the Corporation bought the 18th century villa and its
surrounding parkland from Thomas Molyneux, intending to open
it for public use. But money was short and work did not start until
1868 when the house was converted into a Judges' Lodgings to
provide accommodation for them when they attended the
Liverpool Assizes. Sheil Park, which adjoins Newsham Park, was
started in 1856 and Wavertree Park laid out with trees and
grass in the same year. Newsham Park in 1868 was part of a
three-park policy along with Sefton and Stanley Parks, but very
much the poorer cousin. One can see this in the architecture.
Not only were the houses that surrounded the park nearly all
semi-detached, but park gate posts were economical brick
structures compared to the lavish carved stone and marble
designs for Sefton Park. Nevertheless, Newsham Park has a
charm with its kidney-shaped lake, its circular model boating
pool and its ring of fine trees set in broad grazed fields.

112 Bank Building

1868

60 Castle Street, L1

Architects: Lucy & Littler

A powerful Victorian office block on the corner of Castle Street and Derby Square,
originally the head office of the Bank of North Wales, recalling Liverpool's former
importance as a great regional financial centre. Built on five storeys, the main facade
has seven bays with an elaborate entrance bay with pilasters carved with swags. In the
middle of the second floor, two round-arched windows with iron balconies have the
prow of a ship projecting from the spandril supported by reclining figures. Notice too
the panelled chimney pieces each with its own cornice. An early example of
commercial pomp! It is now called the Trials Hotel.

113 St John the Baptist Church
1868-70
West Derby Road, Tuebrook, L6
Architect: George Frederick Bodley

Pevsner describes it as a 'plain, unshowy, but dignified and sensitive building, and it lies parallel to the road. It is of red stone and has a west steeple, long nave and aisles, a clerestory and a lower chancel. The spire is bluntly recessed'. We might think it more impressive and agree with Charles Locke Eastlake who, in 1873, wrote, 'For correctness of design, refined workmanship, and artistic decoration, this church may take foremost rank amongst examples of the Revival'. It is one of the most impressive of the suburban churches, particularly its interior, and a significant building in both the development of late Victorian church architecture and the emergence of Bodley's style, which reaches maturity in the Lady Chapel of the Anglican Cathedral. George Frederick Bodley (1827-1907) was a pupil of George Gilbert Scott who, combining ecclesiological knowledge with sound taste, continued the tradition founded by Pugin, Scott and Street. The church contains fine painted decorations and wall paintings by CE Kempe with overtones of William Morris, a fine rood screen and windows by Morris & Co, and the interior is thus quite magnificent. The vicarage is also by Bodley.

114 Church of St Margaret

1869

Princes Road, L8

Architect: George Edmund Street

George Edmund Street (1824-1881), architect of the
London Law Courts (1871) and a member of the
Tractarian Movement, knew the plan requirements well –
an elevated and prominent altar at the east end of a
richly-decorated and wide sanctuary, where all could
see and hear the principal service of the church, the
Eucharist. A well-lighted west end with a font in a
prominent position. The emphasis was on baptism and
the Eucharist. The church demonstrates Edmond Street's
love of brightness, and stencilled flower designs are used
extensively. Rich marbles abound. The redeeming feature
which makes it so well worth a visit is the richness of the
interior, which has been partly restored to its original
brightness. There are extensive stencilled decorations on
the walls and the roofs by Maddox & Pearce. A brass
memorial in the chancel to the founder of the church,
Robert Horsfall, recalls closely Street's design for the
memorial to Sir G Scott in Westminster Abbey. The
adjoining vicarage, a rather dull, drab building, is also
by Street. The future of the church is precarious. A
building of this quality must be safeguarded and
preserved.

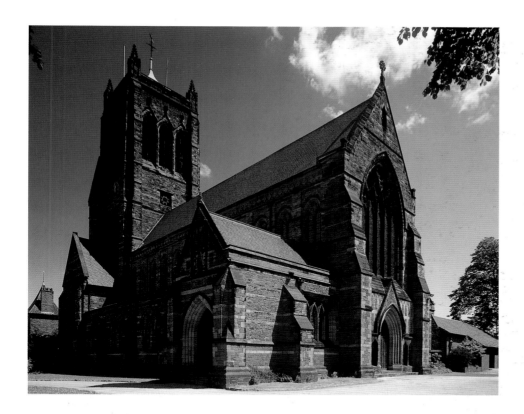

115 Church of St Matthew & St James

1870-75

At the top of Mossley Hill and the junction with Rose Lane, L18

Architects: Paley and Austin

Pevsner considered that, of all the architects engaged in church architecture in Lancashire, only one had genius – HJ Austin (1841-1915). He became Paley's partner in 1868 and together they designed numerous churches in this part of the country. The Mossley Hill Church is one of their best. 'Paley and Austin's towers are handled with great majesty, and their interiors have in all their best designs a completely unexpected, asymmetrical composition of chancel, transepts, and chancel chapels or aisles.' A large robust church typical of their work, its tower dominating the distant view over Sefton Park, it is certainly one of the best Victorian churches in Liverpool. Designed mainly in the style of late 13th century Gothic architecture, it is nevertheless full of ingenious devices and spatial arrangements. The nave was damaged in the blitz when many of the windows were destroyed including work by Henry Holiday. There is an interesting vicarage built in 1873 by the same architects.

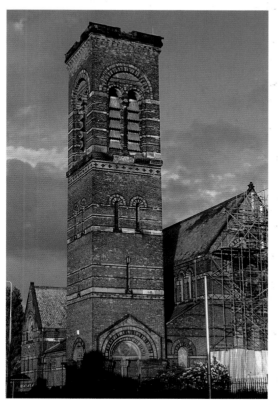

116 Christ Church

1870

Kensington and opposite Ingrow Road, L6

Architects: W & G Audsley

Sadly, this church has been made redundant and its future is uncertain. It is now being used as a furniture store. Designed in the North Italian Romanesque style in common brick with red and blue brick decoration, it has a very tall free-standing tower on the north-west and this was originally topped with a steep pyramidical slate roof.

Everywhere, there are round arches, in the nave on polished granite shafts and deep set in polychrome over the entrance door. It is a large fine building but difficult to use as anything but a church – one of the problems of redundancy.

117 Central Institute of the Mersey Mission to Seamen

c1870, opened 1884
Now Church House
Hanover Street, L1

A fine curved facade in coloured glazed brick – red and yellow – with some rich terracotta mouldings. It forms one of a fine group of terracotta and brick buildings at the junction of Hanover Street with Duke Street and Paradise Street. The five-storey Victorian block opposite, designed to house offices and provide warehouse space, is equally fine with triple-arched brick openings on the ground floor modelled on ancient Rome. For its original use as a haven for seamen, the Central Institute was situated near to the main south docks, the Victorian red light district around Duke Street and adjacent to John Cunningham's now demolished Sailors' Home [72].

118 North Western Hotel

Opened 1871
Lime Street, L1
Architect: Alfred Waterhouse
Architects of the conversion: Owen Ellis Partnership

Originally built as a 330-room station hotel on seven floors, it was later used as railway offices and has now been splendidly converted into students' accommodation for the Liverpool John Moores University – a wonderful new use for an old building. The exterior is Caen stone dressed with Stoureton which gives it a sombre appearance and contrasts with Waterhouse's usual exteriors in Liverpool which were faced in brick. If Liverpool University epitomises the 'Red Brick University' in Waterhouse's Victoria Buildings [136], the John Moores can fairly claim through this use of a Waterhouse building, the title of 'Grey Stone University'. Its silhouette is spiky and romantic, if somewhat out of place in the context of the civic magnificence of St George's Hall and the other classical buildings on the Plateau. However, it has been there long enough for us to accept it and almost love it.

119 All Hallows Church

1872-76

On the junction between Allerton Road
and Greenhill Road, L18

Architect: GE Grayson

A red sandstone Perpendicular Gothic
memorial church built by John Bibby of
Harthill in memory of his first wife. She
was the daughter of Jesse Hartley who
designed the Albert Dock Warehouses.
The church; which is a very early essay in
the Perpendicular style, has a powerful
buttressed tower and contains stained
glass windows by Edward Burne-Jones
and one of the best collections of William
Morris glass in the country.

120 Walker Art Gallery

1873-77

William Brown Street, L1

Architects: Sherlock and Vale

The least impressive of the civic buildings on William Brown Street, but valuable as part of the remarkably coherent whole. Its facade consists of a rather pompous Roman temple hung upon a partly rusticated ashlar facade, interrupted at irregular intervals by Corinthian pilasters. But the contents are magnificent. It is particularly rich in Italian primitives and undoubtedly forms one of the great art collections of the country. The original design was by Vale, enlarged in 1882 by Cornelius Sherlock and again in 1931 by Sir Arnold Thornley. Since the war the galleries have been modernised. In front are seated the monumental sculptures of those two Renaissance giants, Michelangelo and Raphael.

121 Seamen's Orphanage

1871-74

Now Park Hospital

Orphan Drive, Newsham Park, L6

Architect: Alfred Waterhouse

The Institution was founded in 1869 to feed, clothe and educate the destitute children of seafaring men. There was no restriction on nationality but children of Liverpool seamen were given preference. The boys were kept to the age of 14 and then sent into trade, the girls were trained in household duties and stayed there until they were 15. The building was, of necessity, an economy job in common brick, although Victorian economy did not preclude the erection of an almost useless tower and spire. This is a typical Waterhouse silhouette stripped of its usual terracotta decorations. It is now used as the Park Hospital and looks out onto the lake of Newsham Park. However; its future is uncertain.

122 Synagogue

1874

Princes Road, L8

Architects: W & G Audsley

Originally there stood an 'elegant and opulent Jewish synagogue' in Seel Street, designed by Thomas Harrison of Chester in 1807, a building of brick and stone with a pedimented Ionic facade, but, because of pressure for a larger meeting hall, the new synagogue was built in Princes Road. This is another impressive Audsley building in 13th century style but with Moorish overtones. A great rose window above a Norman arched doorway, almost takes over the expression of the facade. It is no reticent statement. The interior is dramatised by the longitudinal emphasis given by the plaster vaulted tunnel of the nave roof. The fact that it was built on a prominent site facing one of the most important radial roads of Liverpool is an indication of the then growing confidence of the Jewish community.

123 YMCA Building

1875-77

Mount Pleasant, L1

Architects: W & G Audsley

Asymmetrical, robust, high Gothic Revival in 13th century style. Not a beautiful building, but one that holds its own and makes no apologies. Characteristic of late Victorian attitudes.

124 Picton Reading Room

1875-79

William Brown Street, L1

Architect: Cornelius Sherlock

A fine drum structure with a peripheral Corinthian colonnade crowned by a saucer dome which, if it creates acoustical problems in the interior, certainly acts as a valuable pivot for the civic buildings at the kink in William Brown Street. The columns stand clear of the main drum of the building, casting, in sunlight, a rhythm of shadows onto its rusticated surface, and the whole building is raised on a full floor podium approached by a double balustraded stairway. In this way the building is able to cope with the fall of the ground which drops quite steeply towards the adjoining Museum.

125 Floating Landing Stage

1876

Pier Head, L1

Engineers: G Fosbery Lyster

In 1874 the brand new £370,000 floating structure, some 2,000ft (609m) long, had not yet been opened to the public when it was consumed by a great fire. Two years later, it had been rebuilt and, added to from time to time, it became the largest floating structure in the world, stretching for nearly half a mile. Very little, save a memory, remains of the original structure. The floating pontoons have been replaced by newer ones, and nearly all the original buildings on it have now been demolished and replaced by modern tent-like ones, the result of an architectural competition. The front is obscured by an ugly block containing, on the first floor, a restaurant.

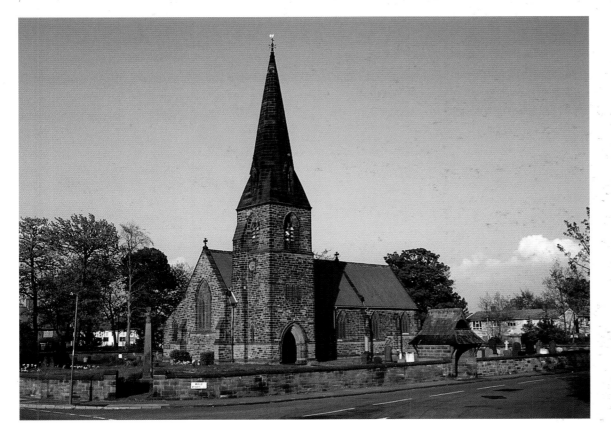

126 Church of All Saints

1876

Speke Church Road off Speke Hall Avenue, Speke, L24

Architect: JL Pearson

Flamboyant Decorated Gothic in red sandstone with red tiles over a timber roof. It has a contemporary lychgate.

127 Steble Fountain

1879

William Brown Street, L1

Sculptor: W Cunliffe

Named after Col RF Steble who was mayor of the city in 1874, this sensuous circular fountain adorned with graceful figures was always thought to have been cast in bronze. It is, in fact, made of cast iron. A cast copy stands in front of the Massachusetts State House in Boston, USA. It looks so much better when filled with tumbling water. Why is Liverpool, and indeed Britain, so careless with its fountains? One has only to go to Rome to see what magnificent architectural effect can be obtained from the imaginative use of water at comparatively little expense.

128 Church of St Cyprian

1879-81

The corner of Durning Road and Edge Hill, L7

Architect: Henry Sumners

Designed by that very individual Liverpool architect. Henry Sumners, unfairly this church has received little recognition. It appears not even to have been listed. Not only is its site important, being on the intersection of one of the ring roads and the main artery from the city to the M62 motorway, but its strangeness is arresting. Sumners has been described as a rogue architect and his work has affinities to that of Medland Taylor in Manchester. All of red sandstone, its tower, containing an entrance arch in the Neo-Norman style, rears up across the west end and is topped by a staircase turret. Inside there is a broad, tall nave with narrow aisles along which are ranged five windows which follow no known Gothic style and are capped by a serried row of gables lighting the interior through the clerestory. It was rerooofed in 1896 so the gables may date from that period. Sumners also designed the Prince's Gate Baptist Church, now gone, and about which Pevsner wrote, 'An astonishing performance, reactionary and at the same time furiously idiosyncratic'.

129 Turner Memorial Home

1881-83

Dingle Road and the end of Park Road, The Dingle, L8

Architect: Sir Alfred Waterhouse

Built as a memorial to Charles Turner, it was intended as a philanthropic venture, a home for old sailors. Unfortunately, the requirement that all inmates must be members of the Church of England and pay seven shillings a week barred the most needy and kept the numbers of the clientele well below the one hundred originally provided for. This need not detract from its architectural merit. Waterhouse may be difficult to love, but this is his domestic work at its best – a splendid assembly of different shaped bits with his usual drum staircase in the form of a turret, little rectangular bands of windows, a bit of half-timbering around the entrance and an ornate frontispiece containing a clock. To the right of the entrance there is a large chapel with high timber roof and a Perpendicular east window. In contrast to the intricate assembly of architectural pieces on the entrance facade, the garden front is rather dull. Unfortunately the building has been sandblasted to remove the soot and the cleaning process has been carried arbitrarily over portions of the tiled roof.

130 County Sessions House

1882-84

William Brown Street, L1

Architects: F & G Holme

The last of the Classical civic buildings in William Brown Street. It is over-ornate and too complicated to be entirely satisfactory, but its sparkling clean stone gives it new attraction. It is a valuable termination to the line of civic splendour.

131 College of Art

1882, extended 1910

Hope Street, L1

Architects: Extension – Willink & Thicknesse

The 1910 extension and refurbishing is the most interesting part of this building. It is carried out in chaste Neo-Grec style, a characteristic of early 20th century Liverpool which seems to draw its cultural ties closer to the United States than to the rest of England, but also to Glasgow. The inspiration is clearly the dynamic influence of Professor Charles Reilly at the Liverpool School of Architecture, and the work is so consistent and integrated that one cannot but feel that he had some direct hand in it. The main entrance, a columnial portico, is deeply recessed into a great slab of flat-surfaced masonry which stands out in front of the building. On each side are two triple-windowed bow windows, almost Regency in inspiration, which might be compared to the end elevation of Reilly's Students' Union [172]. Across the facade the projections are otherwise minimal, giving that classical flatness which emphasised the geometrical form of the buildings in this style. The main hall inside is pure Greek Doric sombreness.

132 Church of St Agnes and St Pancras

1883-85

Buckgham Avenue, Ullet Road, L17

Architect: John Loughborough Pearson

Paid for by Douglas Horsfall, a member of a family remarkable for its generosity and patronage, this splendid church was designed in 1882 in the Gothic lancet style, a style instantly recognisable as by the hand of John Loughborough Pearson (1817-1897). It is a baby Truro Cathedral but without the central tower and spire, and typically Pearson. He does, however, provide a central fleche and two eastern turrets.

But it is certainly not small in scale, Pearson using bold handling of his masses with large plain areas of brick on the outside and stone on the inside. This in itself is strange for most architects would have reversed this alternation of materials. It is also stone vaulted, an expensive expedient not often found in Victorian churches. The interior interlocking spaces are handled with mastery, especially in the relationship between the aisles, transepts and the triforium. It is 19th century architecture in 13th century dress, but still unmistakably Victorian. One of the most impressive churches in the city, admirably supported by Richard Norman Shaw's adjoining vicarage of 1887. The church contains glass by Kempe and work by both Bodley and George Gilbert Scott.

133 Swedish Seamen's Church (Sjomanskyrkan)

1882-83

138 Park Lane, L1

Architect: WD Caroe

William Douglas Caroe (1857-1938) was the son of a Danish consul at Liverpool which may explain how he got the job. Red brick with tall lancet windows, a central octagonal stunted tower with a pyramid roof and a square tower on the south end with a slender tapering oval spire and belfry. In its piled-up form Caroe has produced a fine replica of the traditional Norwegian Stavkirche translated from timber to bright red glazed brick. The interior is equally impressive. The church is a Nordic tour-de-force down by the old Liverpool docks.

134 Prudential Assurance Building

1885-86

Dale Street, L1

Architect: Alfred Waterhouse

Typically Waterhousian Prudential style in red-pressed brick which still retains its original freshness. The asymmetrical tower and the elaborate Oriel window cleverly placed across the corner of the building are also characteristic features of his work. With simplified Gothic windows, comparatively sparse terracotta decoration and a complex rhythm, Waterhouse has made the most of a modest office block. However, the tower was an attempt to attract attention and damn the expense, rather like a child putting up his hand in class.

135 Old Royal Infirmary

1887-90

Pembroke Place, L3

Architect: Alfred Waterhouse

The old Liverpool Royal Infirmary was the third in a succession of four. The first was sited on Shaw's Brow, now the site of St George's Hall, and opened in 1748. By the early 1800s it proved too small, was in financial diffiulties and was now adjacent to a mass burial pit. Demolition was inevitable. In 1824, the second Infirmary was built on Brownlow Hill to the design of John Foster Junior who endeavoured to create a Classical monument containing a spacious, light and airy interior thought suitable for a hospital. During its 62 year life perhaps the most significant developments were as a result of William Rathbone's association with Florence Nightingale. Through her guidance Rathbone established, in 1859, the first district nursing service in the country and, in 1862, a training school at the Infirmary to train Nightingale nurses. The Infirmary also served a steadily growing medical school. Liverpool through the 19th century was prospering and a process of rapid urbanisation was taking place. It was clear that the second Infirmary was ill-equipped to cope. The need to build a new infirmary of inspiration and progress was doubtless seeded in two papers delivered by Florence Nightingale in 1858 in Liverpool, detailing defects in hospital design,

construction, management and practices. She specified the means to remedy the situation and these became the principal guidelines for the future third Royal Infirmary. In 1886 the architect, Alfred Waterhouse, consulted with Florence Nightingale over his designs for the new Infirmary. Indeed, it is not the large Gothic red brick exterior, with its gables and turrets, that appeals, but the beauty of its organisation – a plan that incorporated the now-famous Nightingale rectangular wards and the circular surgical wards. The glazed interiors gave an overall hygienic attraction but were used to considerable aesthetic effect in the chapel where the delicately-varied green moulded tiles adorned the walls, columns, capitals and arcades. The Royal Infirmary, opened in 1888, was admired greatly and continued to function admirably until its closure in 1978 when the new Royal Liverpool University Hospital [206] was opened. In transit, they took as a suitable epitaph from the chapel to the new building, a stained glass window depicting Florence Nightingale, a Rathbone district nurse and a ward sister. For 15 years the old Infirmary has been allowed to decay, but recently there was an inspired plan for the University to convert it into a conference centre, student accommodation, an art gallery and a museum. However, this seems to have given way to a new scheme to use the spaces for a Primary Care Resource Centre, a Clinical Medical Skills Laboratory for students and a Centre for Pharmacological Economics.

136 Victoria University Building

1887-92

The University Precinct,
Brownlow Hill, L3

Architect: Alfred Waterhouse

This and Manchester Town Hall are the masterpieces of the Liverpool born architect, Alfred Waterhouse (1830-1905). The exterior is a clever expression of symbolism and function. The line of the staircase is shown doubling back and climbing into the tower, and the lecture theatre wraps itself neatly behind the cylinder and cone which mark the corner of the building. The interior is equally well handled; the hall is all glazed and from it rises the impressive staircase placed between faienced columns. The whole of the exterior is in hard, red-pressed brickwork and it is in relation to this building that the term 'Red-brick University' was originally coined. As usual, Reilly seeks out its characteristics. 'It leaps up from the pavement with many a spiralling line. In colours of mud and blood it struggles to reach the sky, out Nuremburging Nuremburg itself in its efforts to be picturesque. It has towers and turrets, long Oriel windows, and all the trappings of romance, however expensive, and yet remains the hard prosaic thing we know it to be.' However, when first appointed Roscoe Professor at the Liverpool School of Architecture he was even less enamoured with the building. He said it looked like 'a less prosperous Prudential Insurance building. Its colours of mud and blood and the harshness of its outlines and detail were a great shock after Cambridge and even after King's College, London. It was a greater shock still when I saw the inside of the main block and found I had to teach there. The ground floor and staircase were lined with glazed tiles of the general colour of curry powder, relieved with a narrow line of Cambridge blue. The entrance hall had a Gothic fireplace with a hood over it supported on little arches and columns like an outsize Victorian overmantel modelled in a glutinous mass of the same material.' Our tastes have mellowed since then or perhaps we have become less perceptive and more eclectic.

137 St Agnes Vicarage and Church Hall

1886

Buckingham Avenue, off Ullet Road, L17

Architect: Richard Norman Shaw

Late in the reign of Queen Victoria, that golden age of English domestic architecture, Norman Shaw built this charming little house. It is mainly of brick, with stone mullions and leaded-light windows, and it gains tremendously by its simplicity. With careful handling of the masses and well-judged relationships of features like the Oriel window, the chimney stacks and the wide arched doorway, Shaw has composed his asymmetrical picture, perhaps helped by WR Lethaby who was then his chief architectural assistant. Though small, it is prophetic, a minor milestone in the evolution of the modern domestic style.

138 Deaf and Dumb Institute

1887

Princes Avenue, L8

A curious but satisfying design in bright red hard-pressed brick; it looks like an octagonal church. The architect is not known. It stands at the to start of Princes Avenue, slightly set back as though in apology and somewhat overawed by the impressive facade of the Synagogue [122].

139 Roman Catholic Church of St Clare
1888-90
Arundel Avenue, York Avenue, L17
Architect: Leonard Stokes

This is one of the earliest buildings designed by that most original architect, Leonard Stokes. Edward Hubbard describes the building: 'There is a particularly fine effect of grouping formed by the presbytery and the church with its (liturgically) north transept and octagonal turret with slender spirelet. The presbytery's particular kind of cottage-ish simplicity is unusual for so early a date, as are the art nouveau tendencies of the drip-mould of the east window and the heavy termination of the presbytery door drip-mould. The tracery of the Gothic windows is, however, quite Bodleian and there is little hint of Stokes' characteristic mature style of massive and precise Arts and Crafts Tudor. His individual manner of the 1900s is probably most closely foreshadowed in the semi-circular nave arches inside. A broad nave flanked by narrow vaulted passage aisles which, like the galleries above, cut through internal buttresses.' Had Stokes had his way, the dressed stone interior would have been far superior to the plastered solution which was adopted for economy.

140 Kensington Public Library
1890, enlarged 1897
Kensington, opposite Gwenfron Road, L6
Architect: Thomas Shelmerdine

One of Shelmerdine's fine libraries, it is beautifully composed in an assymetrical manner. It is built of brick and dressed in stone. Above the entrance with its semicircular hood there is inscribed 'Reading maketh a Full man, Conference a Ready man, and Writing an Exact man. (Bacon),' and the roof is topped with a charming white cupola.

141 Adelphi Bank

1892
Later Cooperative Bank
Castle Street, L1
Architect: WD Caroe

Reilly describes this building and its neighbour. 'Then follow two banks on either side of Brunswick Street, both with corner turrets and a great quantity of small, dolls' house detail – hidden away in the corner, there are two bronze doors, full of finely moulded little figures by, I believe, Stirling Lee. What, however, is the meaning of the Rowlands and Olivers, knights and maidens, on a bank door, I cannot tell, though certainly they go well enough with the dolls' house architecture above.' Perhaps he was being a little hard. The allusion to friendly and brotherly love would seem a fitting tribute to a Friendly Society. The bronze doors are certainly magnificent and well worth a visit, and the building itself, with its lively Victorian handling, fits in well enough in this street of such gusto. As a period piece, practically the whole street should be preserved. Some of its interest lies behind its facades and No. 14 Castle Street has a magnificent cast iron staircase in the courtyard.

142 Liverpool Overhead Railway

1893, demolished 1957/58
The Dock Road and along the length of the docks
Engineers: Sir Douglas Fox & James Henry Greathead

Opened in 1893, this was the first electric overhead railway in the world although the New York version, driven by steam, predated it slightly. An elevated steel structure in spans of 50ft and rising 14ft from the surface of the road carried twin tracks some five miles along the line of the Liverpool docks. In 1896 it was extended through a tunnel to the Dingle and, in 1905, northwards to Seaforth and Litherland. Below its decks ran a steam-hauled freight line which, supplementing the heavy carts and horses, hauled the goods to and from the individual docks. Although designed primarily to carry dock workers to their place of work rapidly, the view from the trains was stupendous, opening a panorama of great ocean liners and powerful cargo ships. It must be admitted that the coloured poster produced before the Second World War gave a misleading impression of its scenic value with its deep blue water in the docks and the Mersey. There was never such a tight abundance of ocean liners in such a narrow range of docks and nor did the great ships moor alongside the line of the overhead railway. Sadly, the overhead railway became uneconomical and called for a large sum to repair the rusting ravages of time which had eaten into the steelwork, so, in 1956, it was closed down and soon demolished. Only memories remain which is a shame because, had it been retained there is no doubt it would have become a major tourist attraction.

143 Everton Library

Founded 1895, opened 1896
St Domingo Road, Heyworth Street, Everton, L5
Architect: Thomas Shelmerdine, Surveyor to the Corporation

A fine art nouveau structure built on a triangular site in grimshell and red pressed brick. It was designed to provide a library on the ground floor and a technical school on the first floor and in the basement. There was a segregation of reading rooms – a general reading room, rising through two storeys and illuminated from roof lights. The ladies had their own reading room and so also did the boys. At the opening ceremony it was described as having been built in 'the immediate vicinity of that formerly occupied by a beacon. This beacon guided vessels, richly laden with merchandise up the Mersey, and it is hoped that the building which has taken its place will guide the residents of Kirkdale and Everton to where the rich stores of knowledge lie'. These were contained in 25,000 volumes and the building cost £11,300. Shelmerdine, the architect, was appointed City Surveyor at the age of 26 – the youngest man ever to have been given such an office. He is credited with recommending to the City Council that they should adopt and live up to the motto 'modernise everything'.

144 **Palm House**
1896
Mossley Hill Drive,
Sefton Park, L17
Architects: McKenzie and Moncur

A fine bulbous glass and iron dome, child of the structures at Kew and the Crystal Palace, cocooned its fragile forest of tropical plants. Its crest rises like a white cloud above the trees of the park. Fine art nouveau ravens decorate its iron gates. Sadly, it fell into disrepair and many of its windows were shattered by vandals. It has received a Heritage Lottery Grant and should soon be restored to its full glory.

145 Ullet Road Unitarian Church

1896-1902

York Avenue, Ullet Road, L17

Architects: Thomas Worthington & Son

The Unitarians believe that God is one and that Jesus is a prophet to be followed in his teachings rather than worshipped, a faith they share with Muslims and Jews. From 1811, the Unitarians met in a chapel in Renshaw Street but, by the 1890s, their numbers had swollen to include many of the most prosperous and influential business men in Liverpool, in particular the Holts and the Rathbones. As a result money was found to build a fine new church in Ullet Road facing onto the new Sefton Park. Thomas Worthington & Sons, a Manchester firm of architects who were also Unitarians, were commissioned to design the buildings. The work was undertaken by the younger Worthington who produced a fine Gothic design consisting of a church, a large hall and a linking unit, comprising the lovely library, cloisters containing memorials and a vestry, ranged round three sides of a quadrangle. Ruabon red-pressed brick with red Cheshire sandstone dressings were used outside and the principal interiors are of stone with timber roofs. The church is rich in art nouveau ornament, with beaten copper-faced doors, splendid door handles, elaborate light-fittings and painted ceilings. Within the church there is richly-carved wood on pews, choir stalls, a canopy and a reredos. The ceilings of the vestry and the library are notable, the latter painted as an elaborate allegory of The Triumph of Truth by Gerald Moira. There are stained glass windows probably designed by Burne-Jones and made by William Morris' firm. The linking block contains memorials to notable Liverpool Unitarians such as William Roscoe and Blanco White. The result is one of the finest and most elaborate Nonconformist group of buildings in the country.

146 White Star Offices

Designed 1897
Later the Offices of the Pacific Steam Navigation Company
Now Albion House
James Street; L1
Architects: Richard Norman Shaw and J Francis Doyle

Richard Norman Shaw had already built up a national reputation in architecture when he was called to Liverpool by Joseph Bruce Ismay (1862-1937), son of Thomas Henry Ismay who had acquired the White Star Shipping Line of Australian clippers and built the company into the most important one to ply the North Atlantic. Shaw was asked to help design the interiors of a trans-Atlantic liner. Bruce Ismay later travelled on the ill-fated voyage of the Titanic and his character was for ever tarnished when it was learned that he had been rescued in a lifeboat otherwise filled with women and children. This main office in Liverpool closely resembled New Scotland Yard in London, also designed by Shaw. It is a high-powered office block, part Loire chateau, part Hanseatic warehouse, on a grey stone granite base with a striped superstructure. It is impressive and lively, typical of Shaw's work. Its ornate gable was knocked off by a German bomb but has since been rebuilt in a simpler manner. Although begun slightly earlier than the start of the new century, this is really the first of the 20th century style buildings in the city, the new generation of those giant office blocks which were to transform the appearance of the great cities of the world.

147 Royal Insurance Company Building

1897-1903

North John Street, L1

Architect: J Francis Doyle with Richard Norman Shaw acting as advisory architect. The sculpture is by Professor CJ Allen

From the seven selected entrants for a limited competition, J Francis Doyle was chosen on the recommendation of Norman Shaw, the assessor. Although the drawings submitted were anonymous, it must have been clear to Shaw that the one he chose was by his close friend and colleague, Francis Doyle. Shaw was severely criticised by many but weathered the storm, going on to collaborate with Doyle in the final design and the erection of the building. Probably the innovative steelwork was Shaw's and much of the composition of the building draws inspiration from his work. This is a lofty building some 110ft (33·5m) high and 160ft (48·7m) to the apex of the dome, glittering gold on copper plates catching the eye from many parts of the city. The base is unpolished Aberdeen granite with Portland stone above, richly carved and with close attention to detail. Some of the carved waterheads are 10ft (3m) high. The design is asymmetrical. From the porch you enter a square hall and turn right into the large general office which occupies most of the site at ground level. As this office had to be unobstructed by columns, a novel form of steel construction was devised, a particularly early example of its use in England. The outer stanchions slope in from first to third floor level where arched girders, 34ft (1·36m) apart, occupy almost the whole of the second floor, being hidden in the thickness of the chimney breasts which they support. Panels on the exterior were beautifully sculptured by Charles Allen, a senior lecturer at the Liverpool School of Architecture and Allied Arts.

148 Martins Bank

1898

Deane Road, Kensington, L6

Architect: James Rhind

A very mature little design containing overtones of the later work of Sir Edwin Lutyens. The gables of the building are placed at right angles to each other, and brought together over the entrance which is handled with masterly precision. The interlocking of convex and concave shapes, reminiscent of the Italian Baroque and the work of Francesco Boromini, is here exploited with confidence, while the interweaving of the elements creates a unified solution. It reminds one of a more chaste example of Borromini's church of S Carlo alle Quattro Fontane in Rome. It has now been abandoned by Barclays and is used as offices.

149 Martins Bank

1898

Rice Lane, Walton, L9

Architects: Willink & Thicknesse

Part of Martins Bank policy of employing the best architects on the extensive project of building a number of suburban branch banks. This is one of the best. They all tried to solve the difficult architectural problem of occupying a corner site and facing two ways. The hub forms the entrance and has to be emphasised. It has an ashlar ground floor with brick above, bound with stone dressings and topped with Dutch gables. Although the architectural form is elaborate, it is a beautifully formed and proportioned building very much in the style of Richard Norman Shaw's New Scotland Yard and the White Star Building [146]. Notice how the upper windows on the corner turret are deep sunk like the gun ports on some defensible tower.

Twentieth century architecture

150 **Mere Public House**
c1900
Mere Lane, Heyworth Street, L5

This fine half-timbered pub stands next to the Everton Library and opposite the cast iron church of St George [24]; a splendid group of buildings! It is a particularly good example of the style, robust and vigorous with elaborate, gaily-painted sculpture of wooden Elizabethan figures and painted glass panels. The generous size of the timbers and the mastery of Elizabethan carpentry construction should be noted by those modern architects and builders who now try to emulate the style. The roof line is broken by three elaborate gables, with a fourth placed cleverly on the canted corner designed to announce its welcome presence to those coming out of the library and the church.

151 Martins Bank

c1905

Prescot Road, Derby Lane, Old Swan, L13

Architects: Grayson & Ould

Another of the fine bank buildings built by Martins Bank, classical in style with brick and stone dressings and a Dutch gable onto Prescot Street. On the corner it has an octagonal turret with a concave roof and a lantern.

152 Martins Bank

c1910

West Derby Road, Tuebrook, L13

Architect: J Francis Doyle?

Said to be by Francis Doyle, the architect of the Royal Insurance Building [147] in North John Street, this is in a fine tradition of classical architecture favoured by Martins Bank who maintained a high architectural quality in all their buildings. As usual it has the difficult task of aligning two roads at a crossing and thus having to face two ways.

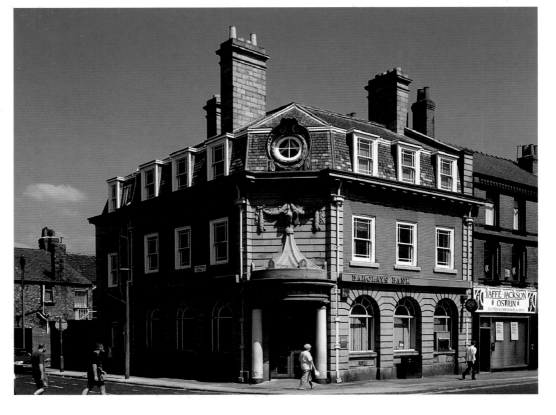

153 Martins Bank

c1900

Aigburth Road, Ashfield Road, L17

Because Ashfield Road joins Aigburth Road at an obtuse angle the wings are splayed and the entrance is tucked between them at the foot of a cylinder which rises to a little dome set beneath stumpy Composite columns – quite a tour de force. The side windows are beautifully detailed with smooth stone voussoirs. As I write, the building is empty and Barclays have it up for sale. What a shame that several of these gems have been abandoned by the bank!

154 Philharmonic Hotel

1898-1900

Hope Street, L1

Architect: Walter Thomas

A labour of love and one of those rich flamboyant demonstrations of the self-confidence of the Edwardian age. It is an art nouveau composition with a particularly rich interior of carved mahogany, cut glass and repoussé copper panels. The plaster caryatid figures in the former billiard room were designed by Charles Allen, and much of the detail was carried out in the workshops of the University College at a time when the School of Art was directly associated with the School of Architecture. The gentlemen's toilet is worth seeing with its marble topped wash basins and their copper taps, and the rich colouring of the tall glazed urinals. Designed by H Blomfield Barr, also a member of the School staff, the bronze gates surely have no equal in the pub architecture of England. Buildings like this are now isolated examples, but when built they formed part of the culture, a setting to which wealthy businessmen had become accustomed and a setting which can still be seen in the old photographs of trans-Atlantic liners which sailed from the Port of Liverpool.

155 Technical School

Project 1898, begun 1902

William Brown Street, L1

Architect: Edward W Mountford

A rather staid work of architecture by the designer of the Lancaster Town Hall. At the lower end of William Brown Street it forms a fitting termination to the great line of classical civic buildings which start with the County Sessions Hall [130]. Mountford's building turns the corner into Byrom Street and in front stand the elegant bronze lampposts designed by his colleague, FW Pomeroy. Look at the delicate details depicting various maritime subjects, beautifully executed and highly decorative. It is to form an extension to the Museum.

156 Extension to the Convent of Notre Dame

c1900

Now adjoining Liverpool John Moores University

Hope Street, L1

A very ingenious extension which wraps itself around an extremity of what was a large late 19th century convent. The crisp quality of the detail and the careful asymmetrical placing of the windows, together with the confidently-placed string-courses lying flush with the brick walls, all suggest a building remarkably in advance of its day, somewhat similar to the work of Mackintosh in Scotland, and one which should be better known.

157 Tobacco Bonded Warehouse
1900

Stanley Dock, Regent's Road, L3

Built on reclaimed ground in the Stanley Dock and obscuring the front of one of Jesse Hartley's Stanley Dock Warehouses [84], this is said to be the largest brick warehouse in the world. Its sheer bulk is impressive, rising through twelve storeys and faced in red and blue brick on a rusticated stone base, it dominates the Dock Road. What to do with it is another matter. It cannot be easy to find alternate use for such a monster but it is a reminder of the scale and impressiveness of line of warehouses which once ran in an almost continuous line to face the miles of Liverpool's docks.

158 Parrs Bank
1900

Castle Street, L1

Architects: Richard Norman Shaw, Willink & Thicknesse

Reilly describes the building well: 'There is certainly no passing it by unnoticed. The colour scheme of the striped marble wall with red terracotta window dressing alone prevents that. But it is, nevertheless, a fine upstanding pile, with its two lower storeys in granite and a strong cornice. The passage of time, however, does not reconcile its strange materials with the street. They are too insistent, and, to be frank, too coarse. The red terracotta dressings to the windows have alone involved this. You cannot get mouldings of the quality, say, of those of the Bank of England and in such material. In the business like reserve of this street, Mr Shaw's building looks to me as some handsome but overdressed woman might look who had strayed there by mistake. The fact that her clothes are slightly soiled, as the marble facing already is, does not really add to her respectability.' Shaw's structural ingenuity comes into play again when he uses steel stanchions to cantilever the back of the high bank building over the roof of the circular hall on a restricted site. He was early in Britain in his imaginative use of steel framing.

159 Toxteth Branch Library

1902

Windsor Street, Upper Parliament Street, L8

Architect: Thomas Shelmerdine

A nice little balanced building in modified English Renaissance style, with overtones of art nouveau and windows inspired by Norman Shaw. Typical of a number of libraries designed by the Corporation Surveyor.

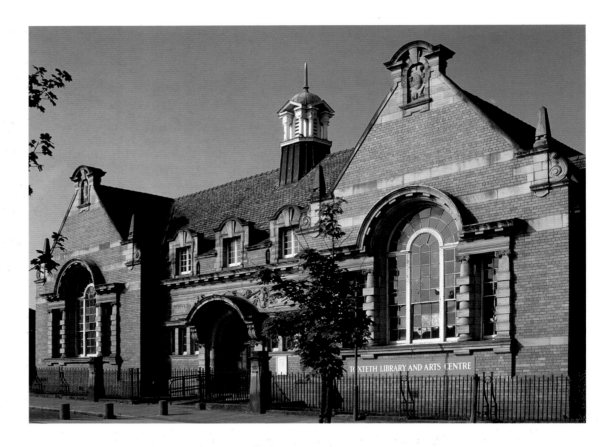

160 Monument to Queen Victoria

1902-06

Derby Square, L1

Architects: Professor FM Simpson, Willink & Thicknesse

Sculpture: Charles Allen

Like many of the Queen's statues, gross, and, in this case, from one angle, obscene. It is nevertheless the epitome of Victorian self confidence. The Queen stands proudly on a pedestal base enshrined beneath a massive dome supported on clustered columns. She is placed on the site of the original Liverpool castle, and a small plaque illustrates it. Although prepared to express such an extravagant gesture of patriotism, Victorian citizens rarely missed an opportunity to provide a functional adjunct, for beneath the stately statue lay one of the proudest public lavatories in Britain; clusters of urinals in white leadless glaze signifying Victorian awareness of the needs of nature. Our own generation has thought fit to remove this underground toilet. By the Second World War this pomposity of a monument was so disliked that students at the Liverpool School of Architecture suggested putting a large sign on the dome – 'Hitler bomb here'. Sadly, the German bombs went astray and destroyed all the surrounding buildings for Victoria's statue seemed to have a charmed life.

161 Anglican Cathedral

1903

St James Road, L1

Architects: Scott & Bodley 1903-7 Sir Giles Gilbert Scott 1907-60
Sir Giles Gilbert Scott, Son & Partners from 1960

The first competition for a new cathedral was disastrous. In 1880 a site was chosen close to St George's Hall and at an awkward angle to it. The Committee stipulated that the building must be in the Gothic style and the prize was awarded to Sir William Emerson for a Gothic design surmounted by a dome. Only then did everyone realise the absurdity of placing two such large structures so close together and, with some courage, for the winner had been announced, the project was abandoned on that site. In 1902 the Cathedral Committee launched a second competition on a new site above St James's Cemetery. They stipulated that the style of the new cathedral 'shall be Gothic'. However, after a storm of objection, they reluctantly rescinded and withdrew this clause and Charles Reilly entered an unsuccessful Classical design. Nevertheless, the bulk of the competitors submitted Gothic designs and the victory was awarded to young Gilbert Scott, then only 23 and a Roman Catholic. Because of the youth of the successful competitor, GF Bodley, the main assessor, was appointed to 'hold his hand' and much of the design of the Lady Chapel can be attributed to Bodley. However, on Bodley's death, Scott continued alone, drastically modifying his design, and produced this splendid edifice we see today – the swan song of the Gothic Revival. The assessors referred to Scott's design as having 'that power combined with beauty which makes a great and noble building'. Certainly, his amendments and refinements improved the building considerably. Scott was always an eclectic and in the first half of this century he was still able to draw widely from a body of informed Gothic opinion, but the designs of his later life, particularly the arch under the great tower, seemed to show a restriction in his repertoire and a hesitancy in the face of modern architecture. It is the largest Anglican cathedral in the world, occupying a total area of 100,000sq ft, almost twice the size of St Paul's in London. Arnold Whittick has described it as a building 'with Gothic calligraphy, which departs considerably from traditional Gothic acquiring a character which links it with the classical tradition. It is as if the spirit of Gothic architecture had extended its hands backwards in time to grasp that of Classical architecture'. Scott was appointed honorary lecturer at the Liverpool School of Architecture and, before the Second World War, he used to show students round the new building, pointing out how every detail in the place had been designed and drawn to full scale by himself so that the masons could make zinc templates from his drafts.

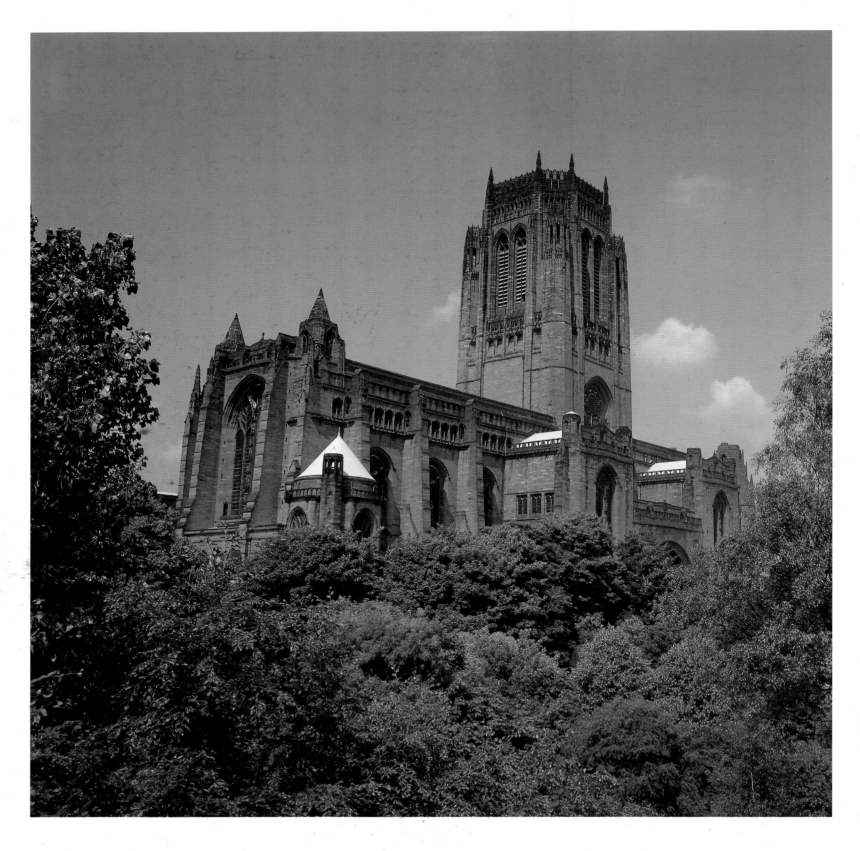

163 Crown Hotel

1905

Lime Street, Skelhorne Street, L1

One of the richest art nouveau exteriors in Liverpool, a pub of gusto and exuberance. It has a base of polished granite and a superstructure of brick, with moulded plaster and gilded letters. It has deep cut glass windows, and beaten copper panels, which pick up the evening light, reflecting it in glittering patterns. If the visitor is still thirsty he, or she, is recommended to go to the Central Hotel in Ranelagh Street, which has a wonderfully rich art nouveau interior – green-tiled dado, acid-edged and brilliant cut mirrors and a rich dome. The smoke room, largely lined with ornate mirrors, is a dazzling gin palace.

163 Martins Bank
1905

Prescot Street, Moss Street, L6

Architect: J Francis Doyle

One of the many well-designed branch banks of Martins and the Bank of Liverpool built at the beginning of the century. It serves the difficult problem of facing two ways and allowing a splay for the site lines at the corner of two traffic routes. It is a miniature Baroque palazzo built at a time when banks had both the taste and the money to spend on good architecture. The Borromini-like lantern is gracefully recessed on each of its eight sides and has no function other than to express the solidity and the power of the banking world; no bells peel across the city roofs for it is just a happy visual statement.

164 State Assurance Building
1906-65

Dale Street, L1

Architect: W Aubrey Thomas. New block by Edmond Kirby & Sons

Part of Thomas's original facade has been demolished to make way for the new office block, but the original composition is not ruined, only broken in half, and the lively art nouveau stone facade acts as a foil to the plain mirror surfaces of the extension. Its graceful Gothic details are quite different in style to the work Aubrey Thomas was to produce later on the Tower Building [166] and the Royal Liver Building [170]; one finds it hard to believe they are all by the same architect.

165 Cotton Exchange

1906

Old Hall Street, L3

Architects: Matear & Son

The ornate Classical Edwardian facade has been demolished and replaced by a new office block, but the original side elevation still remains. These are interesting examples of the continuing use into the 20th century of cast iron as a cladding material consisting of graceful iron pilasters and decorated iron panels; an excellent solution for an office facade.

166 Tower Building

1906

Pier Head, L1

Architect: W Aubrey Thomas

An early example of steel frame construction done by the architect of the Royal Liver Building [170]. Reilly was rude about it: 'The glazed face is dirty in a bedraggled way. A building so clothed is very much like a man with an india rubber collar.' In this case he was a little unfair, as the faienced facade was a largely successful attempt to cope with the soot-laden atmosphere of the city. Except for a skyline of crenellated turrets, a symbolic allusion to the original structure on the site, the old fortified tower of the Stanley family, the building displays plain, undecorated facades with large windows to admit adequate daylight and was, for 1906, a very modern piece of architecture.

167 Walton Stables

1906

Junction of Queen's Drive and Rice Lane, Walton, L4

Architect: John Alexander Brodie, City Engineer

Liverpool seems to have been the first city to use prefabricated reinforced concrete construction. Brainchild of the City Engineer, Alexander John Brodie, it was invented to solve the problem which even at the beginning of the century was assuming gigantic proportions. Anything which would reduce the cost of house construction would be a boon. Liverpool desperately needed houses or flats to shelter the growing numbers of immigrants who flooded in from the countryside of Scotland, Ireland and Wales. The system of using large factory-produced panels was designed in 1903 and first used on flats at Eldon Street in Liverpool, now demolished. It proved an economic failure solely because of labour and trades union disputes, and was only used once more in Liverpool, in these stables at Walton, now much modified and disfigured. But the panels can still be seen at the back adjoining the marshalling yards. So Liverpool lost the lead, through lack of foresight, and has now had to import from France, in our own day, the descendant of this original system.

168 Vines Hotel

1907

Lime Street, Copperas Hill, L1

Architect: Walter Thomas

Walter Thomas at his most ebullient and Edwardian Baroque at its finest, with a splendidly ornate exterior of carved stone, glass and polished brass; it roars up into the sky with a flamboyant tower of quite useless proportions. This tower only contains a tall, thin room. What could one do in a room of those proportions? Still, the brewers were prepared to pay for such excesses! The rich mahogany caryatids and the beaten copper bar are noteworthy. The cocktail bar, especially designed to take Walker's favourite paintings, for he was a great collector of large-scale Victorian art, still holds some of these fine Victorian pieces framed within carved timber and moulded plaster. A splendid setting for the Bacchic bout.

169 Mersey Docks and Harbour Board Building

Completed 1907

Pier Head, L1

Architects: Sir Arnold Thornley with Briggs
& Wolstenholme

The first of the three buildings which form the Pier Head group. An impressive pile of Portland stone: the base, Italian, the superstructure a giant Classical church dome supported by a cluster of little domes. We have grown so used to buildings that perhaps, in our own day, we overlook the underlying symbolism of this form of architectural expression. Could it be that the architect intended the implication that those who worked there combined the business acumen of the Florentine bankers with the sanctity of the Church – a Renaissance merchant's palace with the dome of St Peter's perched on top? The Corporation intended that the adjoining site be developed in a similar manner, but the wily lawyers of the Royal Liver Insurance Society circumscribed the clause allowing their architect the freedom of design which he was to exploit in that most original of structures, the Royal Liver Building. How fortunate was this step, for it has given Liverpool its characteristic skyline and its best known group of buildings. One Mersey Docks and Harbour Board building is splendid, two would have been unutterably boring!

170 Royal Liver Building

Designed 1908, completed 1911

Pier Head, L1

Architect: Walter A Thomas

Reinforced concrete engineers: E Nuttall & Co of Trafford Park, Manchester

'For the architect', writes Reilly, 'this is a mass of incongruities, but to the man in the street rather it is a romantic pile. A mass of grey granite to the cornice, it rose into the sky two quite unnecessary towers, which can symbolise nothing but the power of advertisement. It is only a hard-headed businessman who can waste money in this light-hearted way. It appears that if you promise him a clock that is bigger than any in the world, he will build not one, but a couple of unnecessary towers in which to house it. Yet the building, towers and all, with its coarse and commonplace detail, has a certain grim force combined with its romantic character. In place of elegance and refinement, it offers to the world a bold sentimentality not unlike some north country types of people. It seems to say, "I am a great awkward sentimental creature, unused to civilization, but I have strength, and whether you laugh at me or not I shall get what I want". If I may venture on a comparison, the Liver Building is as obviously plebeian as the Cunard is patrician, even if a little doubtful of its descent, whereas the Dock Board, because it appears to use clothes which appear by tradition to belong to another walk of life, one might, perhaps, without offence, call nouveau riche.' It could never be easy to design so complex an exterior and, inevitably, strange things happen. For example, the superstructure of the Art Nouveau towers looks fine when viewed from the front or the side, but seen obliquely its appears to be sagging under its own weight, collapsing into the stage below. The building is, as one might expect, eclectic. The entrance facing the river is modelled on the Hellenistic temple at Baalbek, probably inspired by a photograph in an architectural history book. The arched window heads, which spring from tall, plain pilasters rising the height of the side elevations, clearly come from the work of an American contemporary, HH Richardson who, in 1885, had incorporated the same devices on his Marshall Field Wholesale Store in Chicago; another example of the close aesthetic links between Liverpool and the States. But besides providing so striking and unforgettable a symbol of the city, the Royal Liver Building has yet another claim to notoriety. Despite its outer cladding of grey-black granite, which gives all the appearance of solidity, it is in fact one of the first large scale reinforced concrete buildings in the world, and certainly the first in Britain; it is held up by a frame. Here we see the start of a system of construction which, along with the development of the steel frame, was to revolutionise the scale of architecture, making possible the tall skyscrapers of the 20th century. A competition to design and make the great Liver Birds was won by a German sculptor and wood carver from the Black Forest, Carl Bernard Bartels (1866-1955), who had come to England at the turn of the century and settled in London. It is interesting to note that little is known of the designer of what has become the imaginative symbol of this city for, when the Great War broke out, he was arrested as a German citizen and incarcerated in the Isle of Man. At the end of the war he was forcibly repatriated to Germany, his wife not being informed, and it took him a number of years and considerable difficulty to get back to England. But, in a fit of xenophobia, it would seem that all references in the local press to his achievement were destroyed and, in Liverpool, his name passed into oblivion. Several Germans suffered this fate. Robert Petsch, the Professor of German at the University, was painted out of a large portrait of the Professors of the Faculty of Arts when the war broke out, leaving an unnatural void in the centre of the picture.

171 City Building

1909

Old Hall Street, L3

Frederick Frazer has refaced an earlier building, providing large areas of plate glass hung between thin cast iron frames. The introduction of curved plate carries the eye around the corner of the building and it lends a Mendelsohnian quality to the design; Eric Mendelsohn, of course, not the musician. The face-lift improved the lighting conditions of the offices and demonstrates the continuity in cast iron constuction in the city.

172 University Students' Union

1910-12, extended 1937 & 1993

The University Precinct, Bedford Street North, L7

Architect: Professor Charles H Reilly, and later Professor Lionel Budden

Then Richard Sheperd and finally, Dave King & Rod McAllister

The original proposals for a Students Union in Ashton Street, made in 1907, were abandoned and in 1909 Charles Reilly, the Professor of Architecture, made new proposals for a fine building between Bedford Street and the curved end of Mount Pleasant. The result was Reilly's own brand of Greek Revival with the hint of an Italian Renaissance palazzo he had helped to father in the city. It is here shown at its most elegant best. It was Reilly's opportunity to demonstrate that a university professor could practice as well as teach architecture, something in which he believed strongly. There is beautiful handling of Greek detail, both inside and out. The Union Building once stood above the cutting which carried the begriming steam engines up the steep incline from Lime Street Station, belching out corrosive smoke. With the introduction of electrification, the railway cutting has been covered and this charming facade cleaned to reveal its pristine brickwork. From a rusticated Florentine stone base, for the ancient Greeks never had this problem, there rose a piano nobile, an expression of facadism hardy justified by the internal plan requirements. Reilly acknowledged the help of his assistant, HA Dod, who was later to design the Harold Cohen Library [193] for the University. The Union was extended between the wars by Professor Lionel Budden with a rather dull, plain addition, for Budden was no inspired architect but a good teacher and organiser, and again in 1961 when Richard Shepherd added a large wing to make it the biggest students' union building in Britain [202]. In 1994 Dave King and Rod McAllister refashioned much of the interior using computer-aided design, but with the fine eye of good architects. The result is spatially exhilarating with inexpensive details that come from that clear understanding that all the constituent parts of a work of architecture are interrelated. Architecture does not have to be expensive, it just has to be good. Outside, Reilly's building is certainly the most notable part. The elegant Regency bow window on the Mount Pleasant facade is worth looking at – Greek Doric on the ground floor with elongated cast iron columns above. Reilly was to reuse old iron patterns on this building.

173 Playhouse Theatre

Opened 1911, extension 1966-68
Williamson Square, L1
Architect: Professor Adshead
For the extension: Ken Martin for Hall, O'Donahue & Wilson

This was originally the old Star Theatre, reconstructed by Professor Adshead into a repertory theatre with 10ft (3m) added to the stage and the original twelve boxes replaced by two large ones. Stanley Davenport Adshead had, in 1909, been appointed head of the new Department of Civic within the University School of Architecture where Charles Reilly reigned. Adshead remodelled the auditorium and cleverly converted the old beer cellar under the auditorium into a foyer. This is one of the loveliest theatres in the country, right in scale, comfortable and elegant in detail that is not obtrusive but chaste; a graceful interior carried out with great taste The style is Greek which saw a second revival in the city in the early years of the twentieth century, inspired largely by the teachings of Reilly, the close contact with the United States where the revival was much in evidence, and by the enthusiasm of Liverpool architects and students for so graceful and chaste a style of architecture and interior design. Ken Martin, with Hall, O'Donahue & Wilson, has carried out further modification back stage and added a new entrance and foyer, bars and promenade spaces in, for its day, one of the most exciting new buildings in the city. Great curves of glass sweep out from one corner of the existing facade, linking it to the tower-top restaurant and the curved ends of the Ravenseft development of St John's Market. This theatre extension both compliments the existing facade and stands as a work of architecture in its own right.

174 Adelphi Hotel

1912-13
Lime Street, L1
Architect: Frank Atkinson

Atkinson, designer of ships' interiors and architect of Selfridge's shop in London, here produced a hotel which is one of the first buildings to express the outer wall surface as no more than a thin cladding hung upon a steel frame. The windows are brought forward to the surface of the wall, to indicate clearly that the latter is of minimal thickness. The interior is particularly splendid. Once the terminal hotel for the prosperous transatlantic trade, it provided luxury for the wealthy passengers. It still has an impressive foyer decorated with mottled marble, and, at the head of a monumental flight of stairs, a splendid palm court where afternoon tea could be taken to the strains of a string orchestra.

175 University Faculty of Arts Building

1913

The University Precinct, Ashton Street, L3

Architects: Briggs, Wolstenholme, Thornely and FW Simon

The design was probably by Frank Simon, architect of the demolished Edwardian baroque facade of the Cotton Exchange. When newly erected, the Arts Buildings caused a tremendous controversy. Cheek by jowl with Waterhouse's Gothic Victoria Building, it was an audacious step to design in an uncompromising Classical style.

176 Cunard Building

1914-16

Now Customs & Excise

Pier Head, L1

Architects: Willink & Thicknesse with Mewes & Davies

The third building of the Pier Head group; six floors of offices for the Cunard Steamship Company on an approximately rectangular site with cross axes on the ground floor and two large light wells providing top light to the main shipping hall and shared by the general manager's and freight departments. On the upper floors the light wells provide cross light to the offices in the H-shaped plan. The style is basically Italian Renaissance; the battered base and the introduction of Greek detail is excused by reference to Baldassare Peruzzi's Italian Renaissance work. The result, seen in historical perspective, is, however, a work of the classical Greek Revival inspired by contemporary architecture in the United States and by Charles Reilly's teachings and propaganda at the Liverpool School of Architecture. In spite of the mixed metaphors, it is indeed a noble building. In front of the main entrance onto the Pierhead stands Henry Pegram's memorial to the staff of Cunard who were killed in the First World War. The architects wished to have a memorial in keeping with the design of their building so, as a result, the solution is rather insipid; sculptors rarely enjoy falling in line with architects' work. It consists of a Roman Doric column raised on a pedestal. Two ship's prows project from the surface of the column, an inappropriate allusion to Roman naval victories in the Punic wars. The only other reference to the splendid maritime activity of the Cunard is the suspension of a slim anchor from the mouldings of the capital. The column is crowned by the figure of Victory, intended by the sculptor to be nude but required by the company to be draped with a fig leaf. The three buildings, the Dock Board, the Cunard and the Liver, make as disparate display of architectural styles as do those around the Piazzetta in St Mark's Square in Venice. There is no attempt at 'keeping in keeping', yet we, with our eclectic tastes, have grown to accept and even love both the group in Venice and that at the Pier Head.

177 Statue of King Edward VII
1916-21
Pierhead, L1
Sculptor: William Goscombe John

On the last of Liverpool's splendid equestrian statues and probably the best; the King is dressed in martial uniform with flowing plumed headgear facing the fierce winds from the Mersey. The bronze horse stands as though bracing itself for this onslaught. A splendid foreground for the famous trio of office buildings, it places them in context and gives them a true scale. Goscombe John also designed the nearby granite Memorial to the Engine Room Heroes which was originally intended to honour those who lost their lives on the Titanic, but later extended to include all engine room crew who were lost at sea.

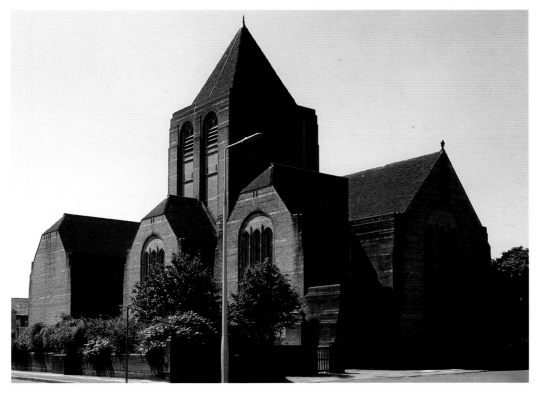

178 St Paul's Church
Designed 1916, built 1922
Derby Lane, L13
Architect: Sir Giles Gilbert Scott

A beautiful early church in silver tone brickwork by Sir Giles Gilbert Scott. Scott's love of plain surfaces comes out. He had shown this in the Anglican Cathedral, particularly in the competition drawings. A critic might say that it was caused by a lack of decision and an inability to do anything with those surfaces. But as he developed he was able to use plain walls tellingly to offset the decoration of window mouldings. Arnold Whittick describes how 'the composition of the exterior is of essentially triangular form, of pitched roofs and pyramidical spire surmounting the square tower – and of circular arches that enclose the triple windows and which terminate the recesses of the tower'.

179 Bank of British West Africa

c1923

25 Water Street, L3

Architect: Arnold Thornley of Briggs, Wolstenholme and Thornley

Sir Arnold Thornley, architect of the Cunard Building [176], has here tackled the difficult job of turning a tall, narrow office building into the semblance of a Greek temple. The Greek Revival persisted late in Liverpool, or was rather revived under the influence of Charles Reilly and contemporary architecture in the United States, and the detailing of the attached columns and their attendant decoration is pure 5th century BC. This is one of a number of attempts in the city offices to come to terms with the task of combining mundane stacked accommodation with exquisite detail.

180 India Building

Designed 1923

Water Street, L3

Architects: Herbert J Rowse, in partnership with Briggs & Thornley

A competition success and one of the giant office blocks of downtown Liverpool. Strangely, Giles Gilbert Scott was appointed the assessor. Herbert Rowse was undoubtedly influenced by his travels in America, and Reilly has written: 'The building would not disgrace Fifth Avenue; indeed, it would sit there very happily and those who know most of modern architecture will know that this is very high praise.' He describes this part of Liverpool: 'Water Street is more like a ravine than a street. It is a steep place running down to the sea, and the inhabitants of Liverpool, like the porcine ones of Gadara, use it in much the same way. They either bolt down to the ferries or plunge down into the hole leading to the Mersey Railway.' The office building occupies an entire city block and is pierced by a spectacular vaulted arcade lined with small shops. It is constructed on a steel frame and faced with Portland stone. It was badly damaged by German bombers but Rowse gladly stepped in and repaired the damage. Herbert Rowse was the most influential Liverpool architect of the inter-war years, although he was not always appreciated by his peers, especially those who espoused the International Modern style of architecture. In 1905 he had been a student at the Liverpool School of Architecture, obtaining a Certificate in Architecture two years later, and he came within the aura of Professor Reilly. However, he was an architect with a mind of his own and would mould his own particular style of architecture. Rowse was a perfectionist, proud of saying: 'Never present an alternative; it shows you have not solved your problem.'

181 Mersey Tunnel

1925-34
Kingsway, off Manchester Street, L1
Architect: Herbert J Rowse
Engineers: Sir Basil Mott & JA Brodie

Reilly complained that they had put the 'hole' in the wrong place in relation to the axis of St George's Hall and that the architect, Herbert Rowse, had been given an impossible task, saying 'The engineer too often feels he can cover up his mistakes by calling in an architect to add pretty things to hide them'. Rowse's distinctive modernistic style is apparent in all the details. He designed the lining of the tunnel which originally consisted of a dado of black (actually dark purple) Vitrolite glass framed in stainless steel. The thick black drum of the lighting pylon which marked the entrance to the 'great maw', that three-mile hole which surfaces again at Birkenhead, is particularly characteristic of the architect's attempt to forge a new decoration in an age in which avant garde designers had discarded the very idea.

182 Cenotaph

1926-30
St George's Plateau, Lime Street, L1
Architect: Professor Lionel Budden
Sculptor: H Tyson Smith

An unusual design for a First World War cenotaph, much lower and more spreading than most, its shape dictated by the long lines of the east facade of St George's Hall which forms its immediate backcloth. The inner facade of the cenotaph contains a long inset bronze panel of solemn marching soldiers, austere and dignified in their bearing, creating a fine unified procession held together by the rigid Classical frame of Budden's symmetrical block. On the other side, and in a similarly-shaped panel some 31ft in length, mourners in simple clothes solemnly gather around a stone of remembrance with, on each side, the serried rows of soldiers' tombstones.

183 Martins Bank Building

Designed 1927, built 1927-32
Water Street, L3
Architect: Herbert J Rowse

On an important site next to the Town Hall, Rowse once more won the competition. With the complex planning requirements the architect was in his element. This is a completely ducted office block, free of exposed pipes or wires with every pipe accessible where necessary. It is also an early example of low temperature ceiling heating. But most of all it is a rich, powerful, decorative building of considerable distinction and quality. Rowse persuaded his clients that an expensive building was a good investment. The banking hall is an extravagant display in Travertine and bronze, and every detail in the building down to the smallest item was designed by Rowse's office. The plan is symmetrical with four corner rotundas and has a large, unobstructed central banking hall lit from above. To achieve this, he had to cantilever the walls of the light well from the sides of the building. The critic in the Architects' Journal wrote: 'It is interesting to note, as a sign of the times, the frank disregard of architectonic construction in the means of pushing the upper floors back from the lower facades. Of course, with steel frame construction there is not the slightest difficulty in supporting walls over voids, and in this case, the economic advantages gained are a measure of justification. All the same it does give a shock to see a wall 60 or 70ft (18-21m) high standing over space and the question inevitably arises: is this architecture or is it not?' But later he reconciles himself to the situation and writes that this is 'probably the best building of its kind in the country. The sugar icing which covers the steel frame, too, is very prettily done with more knowledge and a more consistent sense of skill than is usual in these buildings based entirely on tradition but stretched out to modern size'. On the top floor there is a banqueting hall of great distinction, with medieval overtones but basically decorated with Rowse's own characteristic detailing. He designed all the decoration, even the splendid carpet on the floor. He incorporated the splayed wings of fantastic birds, all gilded, interwoven with formalised bunches of grapes set on a Veridian background. With a suggestion of Egyptian architecture, the overall effect is splendid; it is a fine example of Art Deco decoration.

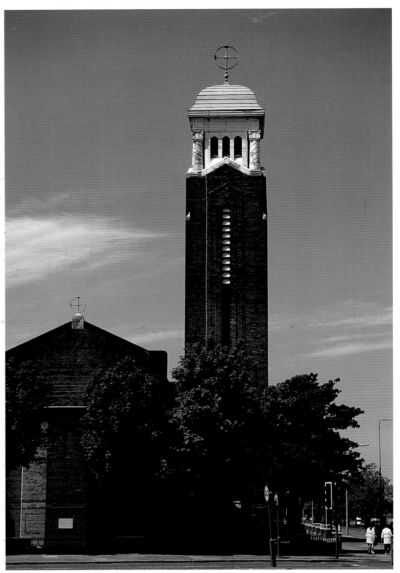

184 All Souls Church

1927

Springwood, Mather Avenue, Allerton, L19

Architects: DA Campbell & EH Honeybourne

A Romanesque church in biscuit-coloured brickwork, very much in the Italian manner with a tall campanile neatly tucked between its arms. The interior is impressive for the uncluttered finish in brick and plaster give it a spacious effect. The double brick arches of the transepts and the vaulted crossing suggest the springing for a dome which is not there. The thickening into six rings of brickwork in the chancel arch is very Roman. One of the best Anglican churches of the inter-war years and done by ex-students of the Liverpool School of Architecture.

185 Roman Catholic Church of St Matthew

1930

Queen's Drive, Townsend Avenue, Clubmoor, L11

Architect: Francis X Velarde

A master of church design, Velarde handled Byzantine Romanesque detail with a new freshness. Nearly all his churches are bold unhesitating statements in this style, equally effective inside and out. There are fine Stations of the Cross by Tyson Smith and a beautiful baldachino and altar. This church, with its attached tower crowned by a small cupola is one of his best. For many years Velarde was a lecturer at the Liverpool School of Architecture and an inspiration to a generation of architectural students.

186 Blackburne Arms

c1930

Catharine Street, L8

Architects: Harold E & H Hinchcliffe Davies

One of a number of fine pubs built at this time in Livepool. This one is beautifully proportioned and detailed to fit in with its adjoining Georgian terraces, an example of 'keeping in keeping' we would do well to study.

187 Crown Hotel

c1930

Walton Hall Avenue East, Stopgate Lane, Norris Green, L9

Architects: Harold E & H Hinchcliffe Davies

How often in Liverpool have the brewers employed good architects to design their pubs and come up with really good architecture which makes a social statement. This pub, with overtones of Neo-Georgian (notice the elegant windows on the end elevations and the fleche on the roof) is a very free handling of the style. The ends are tilted in to embrace the main facade with its continuous first floor balcony and canopy supported on thin iron columns. Yet the building is well in keeping with the excellent Neo-Georgian housing estates designed by Sir Lancelot Keay in that area.

188 Municipal Housing Estates

c1930

Gorse Hey, Queen's Drive, L13

Architect: Sir Lancelot Keay, former Director of Housing

These houses are typical of the vast new estates
undertaken by the City Architect in the inter-war years.
Most of the buildings are Neo-Georgian, but with a very
high standard of finish and excellent siting with open,
American-type gardens. This group in Queen's Drive is
ranged around three sides of a grass square, dotted with
clumps of trees. Lancelot Keay's architecture deserves
more attention than it has had. It is always subtle and
well-mannered, or rather it was before the City sold the
houses to private owners who have, in some cases,
removed the original sash windows and clad the fine
brick exteriors with imitation stone and plastic, in spite of
the fact that these houses are in a conservation area.

189 Forum Cinema

1931

Lime Street, L1

Architects: William R Glen & Ernest Alfred Shennan

The design was done by William Glen and his assistant,
Leslie Horton, but Alfred Shennan's office was probably
used to deal with the building problems in Liverpool.
Shennan was to develop an expertise in Art-Deco
cinemas and public houses. The facade, in Portland
stone, is restrained with meagre decoration applied to the
curved entrance and the two straight wings. But the
interior was plush with elaborate Art-Deco mouldings,
bright colours and concealed electric lights. It was a
dream palace for those who crowded in to escape from
the drabness of their homes and streets. The decoration
was highly inventive, with no trace of Classical
borrowings, in an age when elsewhere avant-garde
architects, fortified by the writings of Adolf Loos,
eschewed all forms of decoration from their modern
architecture. The cinema was opened by the Lord Mayor
on 16 May 1931 when, rising from a pit, the great
Compton organ, flashing with internal coloured lights,
thundered out its music under the expert hands of
Reginald Foort. The large impressive auditorium of those
days was modified in 1982 when the space was carved
up into three separate cinemas.

190 Philharmonic Hall
1933-39, extended 1994-95
Hope Street, L1
Architect: Herbert J Rowse
For the extension: Brock Carmichael & Partners

Rowse, attracted to the middle-of-the-road modernism of the Dutch architect, Dudok, in the thirties, was called to rebuild the Philharmonic Hall after its destruction by fire in 1933. This is a Classical plan of cross axes with a simplified, almost moulding-free brick exterior. His move towards this type of brick expression can be seen in some of the ventilating shafts for the Mersey Tunnel, especially those in Birkenhead. The Philharmonic Hall has a fine acoustical interior – one of the first modelled on acoustical data. It accommodates an audience of 1,760. This dependence upon the Dutch architecture of Dudok was not confined to Rowse. It was found in contemporary flats designed by Sir Lancelot Keay. Nor was an appreciation of Dudok confined to Liverpool; in 1935, he was awarded the RIBA Gold Medal. The hall has now been renovated with the minimum of alterations to the appearance of the auditorium. Additions have been made at the back and along the sides in a style that shows some sympathy for the Dudok style of the original building.

191 City Airport

1933-37
Speke Hall Road, Speke, L19
Architect: R Arthur Landstein, Chief
Architect in the office of Albert D Jenkins,
City Surveyor

The airport was opened in July 1933, and the symmetrical terminal building, completed in 1937, stands like a lighthouse, flanked by monumental hangars set at splayed angles to the main front. It is probably the first airport in Britain to be designed to represent symbolically the shape of aircraft, and one of the first purpose-built airport terminals in the world. Sir Alan Cobham who, in the thirties, was famous for his flying circus, is said to have advised on the design. It is also the first municipal airport building in Europe. The two hangers are also important for they form part of the grand composition and are beautifully designed and detailed with lively little pieces of sculpture placed here and there. The interior was modernised in 1963 and a new block built at the back by the City Architect, Dr Ronald Bradbury. Sadly, this terminal building is now empty as a new metal shed has been put up to house passengers nearer the end of the new runway. That shed is a sad reminder of Liverpool's present architectural paucity.

192 George's Dock Building

Opened 1934

Pier Head, L1

Architect: Herbert J Rowse

This stately tower hides the main Liverpool ventilating shaft for the Mersey Tunnel [181]. Begun in 1925, the tunnel in itself is nearly three miles long and was opened in 1934. The architecture of the tunnel mouths, the monumental lamp standards, and the other ventilating shafts are all by Rowse. This building was badly damaged during the war and was largely rebuilt by Rowse between 1951 and 1952. It is worth looking at the decoration. At a time when most of the young architects influenced by the Modern Movement in architecture were stripping their buildings of all decoration following the dictates of Adolf Loos laid down in his book on *Ornament and Crime*, Rowse was constantly searching for a new form of decoration trying, wherever possible, to avoid

Classical detail based on Greece and Rome. And this was at a time when the Greek Revival, led by Professor Reilley, was returning to Liverpool. Rowse used to go into his office in the morning and set a group of his assistants the task of producing the decoration for a small detail of the building. He would return at five o'clock and select one solution for further development, and so the process of evolution proceeded. This search for decorative solutions gained him few friends in the architectural press but within his office he ruled with an autocratic hand. Perhaps fine in the conduct of architecture but more problematic when he tried to apply this haughty behaviour to his social life in Wales. After the Second World War he bought an old house on Anglesey and soon he was at loggerheads with the locals, trying to deny them access to fields they had visited for generations and from paths they considered their rights of way. In the end he made himself so unpopular with the Welsh that he was driven from the place and forced, with great reluctance, to sell his seat of recluse.

193 St Andrew's Gardens Rehousing Scheme

Completed 1935

Brownlow Hill, Russell Street, L3

Architect: Sir Lancelot Keay & John Hughes

This was a central area inter-war re-housing scheme, designed by John Hughes in 1931, consisting of five floors of high-density flats. Hughes was assisted by Gordon Stevenson, another Liverpool graduate whom Lancelot Keay had recruited to strengthen his design team and who later became professor of Civic Design. To avoid decanting the population, a 50 acre site was chosen for redevelopment where the old Brownlow Hill Abattoir had stood near the town centre. Being close to the town and the docks was an advanced proposal for its time. The total cost for this scheme was £133,450, which gave a gross average cost per flat, including roads and services, of £422. There were 316 flats encircling a large courtyard. Because of its shape, it became known as the Bullring. The style is brick with a Dutch influence of Kramer and de Klerk, and perhaps too, there is an influence from the Karl Marx Hof flats built in Vienna in

1930. Corporation officers visited Vienna shortly before commissioning this project. Keay was much impressed by the 'horseshoe' block of flats in Berlin designed by Bruno Taut and Martin Wagner, which may also have influenced the new design. The original drawings of the Liverpool flats suggest the architects wanted to use plain white surfaces and a flat roof. Exposed brickwork was only substituted because of a chronic local shortage of plasterers. The flat roof was changed to a pitched roof which is hidden behind a high parapet. Notice the bull-nozed stair turrets and the arches. Hughes had used the horizontal banded fenestration before on his prize-winning thesis at the Liverpool School of Architecture. Designed to build a cohesive community within the embrace of the encircling walls with adequate recreation space in its courtyard, St Andrew's Gardens was an audacious scheme, both socially and architecturally, and was largely successful at the time. The main criticism was that the paved courtyards and the high buildings formed a sounding area in which the noise of children's play was greatly accentuated. It is now being sensibly converted into student accommodation and should accommodate them well.

195 University Department of Civic Design
1950-51
The University Precinct, Bedford Street South, L1
Architect: Professor Gordon Stevenson

Part of the post-war development of the University, and the first break-through into the modern style; the initial project having been Neo-Georgian. The main block has a well handled relationship of solid to void, but its link to the criticism room on the side elevation is clumsy. The Department envelops two sides of an urban courtyard containing modern sculpture. It is believed that Fritz Wolff, once a student at the Liverpool School of Architecture, had a hand in the modern design.

194 University Cohen Library
Designed 1935, built 1936-38
The University Precinct, Ashton Street, L3
Architect: Harold A Dod of Willink & Dod

Designed by Harold Dod (1890-1965), a Liverpool graduate and, for a short while, a lecturer in the School of Architecture, the entrance faces an archway leading from the University quadrangle, and contains the main reading room, with the catalogue hall behind it. At the rear, the book stacks, designed to hold 650,000 volumes, are laid out on eight decks. The main facade is somewhat inhibited – emaciated Classical and the sort of building that would have sat happily in Mussolini's Italy – but the rear elevation, with its unflinching expression of the book-stacked floors, is a much more convincing statement. The piece of sculpture over the main entrance was designed by Eric Kennington.

196 Corn Exchange

1953

Fenwick Street L1

Architect: H Hinchcliffe Davies

One of the first large, post-war office blocks, somewhat inhibited by a desire to create a monumental gesture. A hint of the influence of Le Corbusier can be seen in this building, but the master's dynamic gestures have been watered down. Still, it is a brave, if late, attempt to bring the Modern Movement to Liverpool and the building, with its chamfered end facade, has dignity.

197 University Physics Building

1958-60

The University Precinct, Peach Street, L3

Architect: Sir Basil Spence

A cleverly contrived plan by the architect of the rebuilding of Coventry Cathedral and of the British Embassy at Rome. The glass tower block, containing staff and research rooms, straddles the entrance from which leads a long corridor down the main axis of the building. Workshops and laboratories are arranged like ribs on a vertebral column leading to a lecture theatre complex at the other extremity of the building. The various functions of the building are separated and clearly articulated externally.

198 Metropolitan Cathedral of Christ the King

1962-67

Mount Pleasant and Brownlow Hill, L3

Crypt architect: Sir Edwin Lutyens. Architect of Cathedral: Sir Frederick Gibberd

Here once stood the largest workhouse in England. It had been built in 1842 to house 1,800 inmates but was soon expanded and overcrowded to hold 4,000. In 1928, Archbishop Downey purchased the site bounded by Brownlow Hill and Mount Pleasant and here Sir Edwin Lutyens planned his vast monumental pile, intended to be the second largest cathedral in the world. Its mountainous outline drawn from Classical Byzantine sources, was inimitably Lutyens and would have formed a dramatic foil to Scott's Gothic silhouette, the Anglican Cathedral, at the other end of Hope Street. Between 1930 and 1937, work continued on Lutyens' vast cathedral and the stately sombre crypt was built. But war and the expense of the project halted the work. Soon both Downey, the driving force, and Lutyens, the powerful architect, were both dead. All that now remains of that project is the powerful Lutyens crypt and the magnificent model of the whole scheme recently restored and displayed in the Walker Art Gallery. In 1953 the idea was rethought and Adrian Gilbert Scott was commissioned to draw a reduced version of the Lutyens' Classical design. This scaled-down version was an unhappy solution and was mercifully shot. In 1959, Cardinal Heenan promoted an open competition for a completely new solution. Frederick Gibberd's design was selected from the 293 entries. Work began on the new cathedral in September 1962 and the building was virtually complete for the consecration ceremony on 13 May 1967. Gibberd has called it 'a precise geometric structure on a precise, geometric base, growing out of irregular rocky surroundings'. It consists of a drum of concrete columns, hooped by three massive ring beams and pinched in to a tall, lace-like lantern whose crown towers 290ft (88m) above the ground. The beams between the two lower rings continue diagonally to the ground, forming exposed flying buttresses between which are assembled the Chapels of the Saints, the Chapel of the Blessed Sacrament, and the entrance porch. The giant cone of the cathedral has been cleverly placed, resting on a podium formed by the roof of Lutyens' crypt. Although the approach from Mount Pleasant is partly obscured by what was originally the University Nuclear Physics Building, this structure is eventually to be demolished making way for a straight flight of steps from the street to the entrance. The entrance itself lies beneath the upended triangle of the bell tower, which, facing out from the cathedral, rests on the triangular wedge of the entrance porch. The fact that it has become the subject of innumerable jokes suggests that it has been amiably accepted by the people of Liverpool who already look upon it with affection. Its giant wigwam is splendidly photogenic and the building is undoubtedly the major modern architectural attraction of the city.

199 University Mathematics Building
1960

The University Precinct, Bedford Street North, L3

Architects: Brian and Norman Westwood

The plan is reminiscent of a French chateau. You pass through a gatehouse into a green court then by a drawbridge over a watery moat to the main block. The exterior is broken into a large texture of triangular shapes, the architect intending to get the maximum chiaroscuric effect in this smoky atmosphere. Unfortunately, this has given a fragmented appearance to the building, accentuated by the flippant tilt of the serrated roof pattern and the nearness of the building to the newer Department of Electrical Engineering with its large areas of plain white tile. Two less happy neighbours could hardly be imagined. The lower foreground buildings house the Departments of Oceanography and Numerical Analysis, and the computer was in an air-conditioned cube under a paraboloid roof.

200 House in Beaconsfield Road
1960

Beaconsfield Road, L25

Architects: Gerald R Beech & Dewi Prys Thomas

A little gem of a house, lovingly detailed. The ground floor is brick with a white Tyrolean finish, and the upper storey, timber-framed and clad, forms a cantilevered box. Openings are proportioned and placed with the greatest care both for the internal and external effect. The garden, with its reflecting pool, adjusted ground levels and selected planting, was an integral part of the scheme. Judged the *Woman's Journal* 'House of the Year' in 1960, it certainly deserved the award.

201 University Wyncote Sports Pavilion
1961-62

Geoffrey Hughes Memorial Ground, Mather Avenue, L18
Architect: Gerald R Beech

A fine pavilion block poised gracefully, like a Japanese temple, in a related setting of trees and grass. The pavilion is a glass box cantilevered at first and second floor level, then pinched in above to form a wide viewing terrace protected by the over-sailing flat roof whose edge lines in with the surface of the glass box. The pavilion is linked to changing accommodation by a flying open gallery from which open steps zig zag to the ground. The layout resembles a pier with all the accommodation accessible from an elevated promenade which joins the spine of the scheme. Gerald Beech's Pavilion won a Civic Trust Award and is an outstanding example of post-war modern architecture. It should be listed for its safekeeping.

202 University Students' Union
1961-63

The University Precinct, Bedford Street South, L3
Architects: Bridgewater, Shepherd & Epstein

The extension, tacked on to Sir Charles Reilly's nucleus for the Union [172], made this the largest students' centre in the country. The block provides lounges, restaurants, cafeterias, bars and a large assembly hall, ranged around a central courtyard. The exterior has long sloping roofs on raked brick walls with crisp white windows framed in white faience. The impression is one of amplitude and the lineal features are well disposed and not over fussy. It has now been re-furbished by Dave King and Rod McAllister.

203 University Law, Social Science & Modern Languages Buildings

1962-64

The University Precinct, Cypress Street, L3

Architect: Brian Westwood

The group of buildings form a compact integrated group comprising what was the Arts Library, the Faculties of Law, Social Science and the Modern Language Building. Designed by one architectural firm, they show a consistency in the use of concrete with surfaces of black aggregate played against the pattern of rough timber framework. The smaller buildings are the more successful – the Arts Reading Room and the Law Building.

204 University Arts Library

1962-64

The University Precinct, Bedford Street South, L3

Architect: Brian Westwood

Originally conceived as an arts library to be used in conjunction with the Sydney Jones Library, for which it was well designed. Economic forces have caused its function to be changed, which is a pity. The facades have a plain brick plinth occupying the whole of the ground floor with a piano nobile clad with hanging panels of textured reinforced concrete, its flat roof tilting gracefully up at each end. The rooms are ranged around a courtyard garden, a peaceful spot for contemplation which can be glimpsed through the large openings of the entrances at front and rear. However, with the centralisation of the University libraries sadly this use has been abandoned.

205 University Department of Electrical Engineering & Electronics
1963-66
The University Precinct, Ashton Street, Brownlow Hill, L3
Architects: Yorke, Rosenberg & Mardall

This RIBA prize-winning design is typical of the firm's work, its exterior entirely clad with horizontal white-glazed tiles. Long bands of bronze painted windows, their heads cut back to allow top illumination, divide the five upper floors equally, but the ground floor is on a grander scale, a glass screen encasing the solidity of the lecture blocks upon whose outer walls large modern paintings are hung, visible from the street. The impressiveness of the building is increased by standing it in a dry moat with an approach from the Victoria Buildings over a narrow concrete gangplank. The whole facade forms a disturbing effect at the end of Bedford Street, but from other angles the building appears admirable.

206 Royal Liverpool University Hospital
1965
Prescot Street to Pembroke Place, L7
Architect: Ward Shennan of William Holford & Associates

A vertical filing cabinet for sick human beings. Liverpool brought together four scattered hospitals and sited the new Medical Teaching Centre close to the old Royal Infirmary [135] and the University Schools of Medicine and Tropical Medicine. The new unit is a general teaching hospital with 800 beds made up of 16 x 50-bed units, divided into 25-bed nursing units with certain shared facilities. There are ten operating theatres linked to wards by lifts. The whole scheme was built with in-situ concrete and the character imparted from its formwork intended to form a unity in the architecture. The ward block is the most dominant feature. It rises twelve storeys from a podium, its roof edge being tilted out like a pagoda. The ward design is know as 'racetrack,' in which patient areas are situated around the edge of the block with ancillary and service rooms, routes and corridors forming a central core. The other eye-catcher is the boiler house with its 220ft (67m) high circular fluted flue. The boilers themselves are exposed to view behind large sheets of glass. The theme of the roof edge of the ward block is replayed in the design of the main water tanks which are cantilevered in a tip-tilted structure from the bottom of the chimney. Notice the way in which the size of the ribbing on the chimney diminishes in three stages as it climbs to the apex. Although the concrete facing of the hospital has tended to become drab where it has been stained by the pollution of the city, the mouldings of the panels have been carefully considered and pleasingly arranged. In front of the main block stands the chapel, a massive red brick structure, square, robust and buttressed; in stark contract to the fenestration of the ward block.

207 **Christ's & Notre Dame College of Education**
1964-66
Woolton Road,
Taggart Avenue, Childwall, L16
Architects: Weightman & Bullen

An impressive complex of modern buildings in a well-landscaped setting. The design and detailing is consistent and the climax builds around the chapel, a square laid diagonally across a square, building up to an irregularly pitched roof.

208 **Fulwood Lodge**
1964
Fulwood Park, Aigburth Road, L17
Architect: Nelson & Parker

A long low house with the living area of post and beam timber frame, sandwiched between a load-bearing brickwork bedroom block and a car port of brick piers and timber beams. Each form of structure is used because its characteristics are ideal for the particular requirements, and these are then exploited to strong contrast.

209 Allerton Branch Library
1964-65

Mather Avenue, Harthill Avenue, Allerton, L18

Architect: Dr Ronald Bradbury, City Architect

This is one of a number of new branch libraries built by the Corporation. An elegant single-storey structure, framed to allow large unobstructed space inside, it sits on a triangular site which has been well landscaped with cobbles and paving. The project cost £44,000 and houses 22,000 volumes.

210 University Department of Veterinary Medicine
1965

The University Precinct, Brownlow Hill, Chatham Street, L3

Architect: E Maxwell Fry

Maxwell Fry, one of the pioneers of the Modern Movement in England, was a student at the Liverpool School of Architecture, and it is unfortunate that, of all his buildings, the two he designed for the University of Liverpool are the least successful. His Civic Engineering building was followed by the Department of Veterinary Medicine. The building functions well, but has a drab appearance. To some extent, this was an intentional, though unfortunate, design decision. If you could not beat the grime of Liverpool, you designed to look a part of it. This was, of course, before the Clean Air Act was brought in and much of the smoke was removed. The building was designed to face the open ground of the Science precinct and looks best from that side. Unfortunately, its foreground of grass and trees has now been marred by the decision to place there the Science Lecture Rooms. With the pressure on valuable land, grass has had to give way to structure.

211　University Sports Centre

1965-66

The University Precinct,
Bedford Street North, Mount Pleasant, L3
Architects: Denys Lasdun & Partners

A well conceived sports centre with a central core of changing and ancillary accommodation, sandwiched between the two large halls containing the swimming pool and the games area. At each end raked concrete columns support the tip-tilted roof which slopes in towards the large concrete block of the water tanks cleverly poised over the thin slit which marks the middle of the Bedford Street facade. An elegant prima ballerina of a building dancing on too small a stage, embarrassing the serenity of Abercromby Square into whose corner it intrudes.

212　University Carnatic Halls of Residence

1965-67

Mossley Hill, Elmswood Road, L18
Architects: Manning & Clamp

The halls are named after Liverpool's 18th-century privateering exploit – the capture of the French East Indiaman *Carnatic* in 1778. For, on this site, lived the owner of the ship which made the capture and the recipient of the prize money. The University acquired this heavily wooded site and Manning & Clamp were awarded first prize in an international competition for Halls of Residence. The view from the parkland is good, with dark brick and concrete buildings relieved by clichés (not necessarily bad). The roof of the catering hall is modelled on Le Corbusier's Maison Jaoul, via Sir Basil Spence. The residential blocks are terminated by glass drums engirdled by thin concrete ribs. If at first these appear to be chapels, closer inspection will prove them to be escape staircases. Reflecting pools of water, grass, forest trees and the dark toned buildings make a restful setting which should be conducive to study. The area abounds in halls of residence. On the other side of the road lies Dale Hall by Rolf Hellberg (1958-59), a girls' residence in Scandinavian style. Nearer the city and adjoining Greenbank Park, other halls girdle a fine landscape park. On each side of the Gothic Club at Greenbank House lie University Buildings. The earliest is Derby Hall (1937-39 by Willink & Dod), a strange Neo-Georgian building with an incongruous high pitched roof but mellow, and now absorbed into the area. Next is Rathbone Hall (1958-59 Gilling, Dod & Partners), dull modern, but with a much better yellow brick extension by the late Malcolm Gilling, built between 1960-61. On the other side of Greenbank House lie Gladstone and Roscoe Halls in harsh red brick by David Roberts (1962-64). Less sympathetic to the setting than his college work in Cambridge, they stand as though waiting for a further storey to be added.

213 Conversion of a Stable into a House
1966
Eaton Road, Cressington Park, L19
Architect: Robin Clayton

In this conversion into a two-bedroom house, some of the quality of the old stable is retained. The theme of the curved corner and the circular eye is picked up in the shape of the new windows and the canopy over the door. The south elevation is opened up with large windows and the little building has a light, charming character imparted by white paint, varnished pine and local brickwork.

214 University Science Lecture Rooms
1966-67
The University Precinct, on the site of Peach Street, L3
Architects: Professor R Gardner Medwin
in association with Saunders, Boston & Brock

The building accommodates four lecture theatres, a mathematics reading room and a suite of rooms for the Dean of the Faculty of Science and his staff. The site is a narrow one facing south to the landscaped space of the science precinct and north to the pedestrian way and car park which has been formed by covering over the railway cutting. Foundations had to be kept 10ft (3m) away from the rock side of the cutting to prevent serious vibrations. Steel columns and trusses proved to be the most economical structural solution for the larger theatres, but nearness to the railway cutting prompted the use of cantilevered reinforced concrete construction for the smaller theatres. The resolution of these two constructional systems in a unified aesthetic was a challenge for the architect. The distinction is clearly made, brick infill panels in the former case and large areas of concrete in the latter. The rough plank marks of the formwork are used to give an integrated quality to the whole building and this is carried to the interior. For the internal, non-structural walls, concrete blocks replace brick panels. The design is successful in both functional and sculptural terms. It was designed by the Roscoe Professor of Architecture at the University.

215 Roman Catholic Church of Christ the King

1966-67

Queen's Drive Wavertree, Meadway, L15

Architects: Pritchard, Son & Partners

A lively pyramidical structure on a plain brick base resting on a sloping brick plinth, the joints all raked and neatly executed. One of the best of the modern Catholic churches. The architects seem to have known just when to stop and the building has therefore avoided appearing fussy.

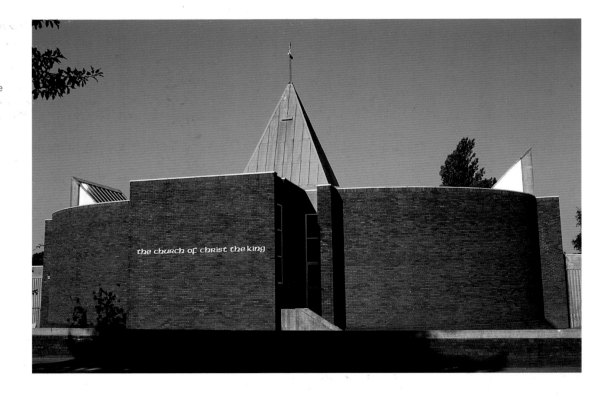

216 Federation House

1966

Hope Street, L1

Architects: Gilling, Dod & Partners

Federation House contained the headquarters of the Liverpool Federation of Building Trades Employers and had the Liverpool Design Centre on the ground floor, and a lecture theatre, display area and information storage for the Building Centre on the ground and first floor. The ground and first floors are constructed with an in-situ reinforced concrete framework giving large uninterrupted areas, and the upper floors are built with precast, prestressed, factory-produced concrete floor and wall units. The H-frame structural units, each consisting of two columns and beams, factory made and measuring 11ft 3in by 10ft 3in (3·4 x 3·1m), weigh one and a half tons. This is the first use of the system in the north of England. Above the ground floor the building is wrapped with a Neo-Aztec band of sculpture by William Mitchell.

217 Piazza Waterfall, Wilberforce House
1966
The Strand, Brunswick Street, behind Wilberforce House, L1
Engineer: Richard Huws

Bronze posts and stainless steel cups of varying size, all worked out mathematically, cascade at intervals into a large black tiled tank. A witty *trompe l'oeil* holds children fascinated for hours. Just what a fountain should do! Let the inventor describe it. ' "What is it? What is it meant to be?" the woman asked. She was one of those who was outraged by the sight of an unfamiliar image; anything that cannot be recognised by its label in the catalogue. Had I said "fountain", she would have exploded, but I said "waterfall", which caught her off guard and, while her thoughts were momentarily switched to Bettws-y-Coed and Niagara, she could not help being dimly aware that the word "waterfall" had some kind of relevance to the spectacle of falling water at which she was staring. It is a waterfall of a strange new kind which instead of streaming steadily hurtles down unexpectedly in detached lumps in all directions. The sight and sound of waterspouts and waterfalls is so spellbinding that they have always been centres of attraction in the landscape and, in the places where we live and work, where they seldom occur naturally, we are prompted to create them artificially in the form of ascending jets or sprays and in the form of descending cascades. Their perpetual bubbling, however, tends to pall after a while and to make it more exciting we contrive various means of providing added animation, such as changing sequences and coloured lighting, or jets and sprays which rise and fall or twist and whirl. Our waterfall is yet another such contrivance; it was conceived as yet another way of adding animation and excitement, but unlike the former expedients it does not depend on elaborate hydraulics or complicated controls; it depends only on a very simple device which interrupts the regular flow so as to create a round of action, the sound and movement of which is no longer that of the monotonous ever burbling river, but that of the restless temperamental sea. There are 20 cascading cups and water enters them through holes in concealed branch pipes which serve also as bearing shafts or axles. The number and size of the holes is different for each cup so as to vary the rate of filling and timing of the cascades. The spent cascades mingle with the reserve water in the pool, from which a pump draws the required amount to replenish the pipes so that water does in fact flow continuously in a circuit.' It was a brilliantly exciting solution to the problem and an asset in a public space in Liverpool. Sadly, it has now been allowed to dry out and no water cascades onto the square. Surely this is something the citizens of Liverpool must insist is once more made to work. It was such fun to all, young and old!

218 **University Senate House and Oliver Lodge Physics Laboratory**

1967-68

The University Precinct, Abercromby Square,

Oxford Street, L3

Architects: Tom Mellor & Partners

The University was given permission to demolish one side of the scheduled Abercromby Square and Foster's Church of St Catherine on the condition that it would retain the other three sides for 15 years. The demolished side made way for Tom Mellor's Senate House. The colour of the brickwork and the roof line of the buildings are attempts at 'keeping in keeping' with Abercromby Square, and this may have inhibited the architect, for the result is uninspired. Worse still is the bridge which joins the Senate House to the Oliver Lodge Physics Laboratory on the other side of Oxford Street. The bridge looks weak and unstable, particularly as the main supporting beam is in the centre, leaving shallow beams above and below, which seem inadequate to support the load. The Laboratories have a robustness and forcefulness which the Senate House fails to achieve, and the view from the Chemistry Building is by far the best. In front of the Senate House and facing onto Abercromby Square stands Barbara Hepworth's sculpture *Squares With Two Circles*, executed in 1963.

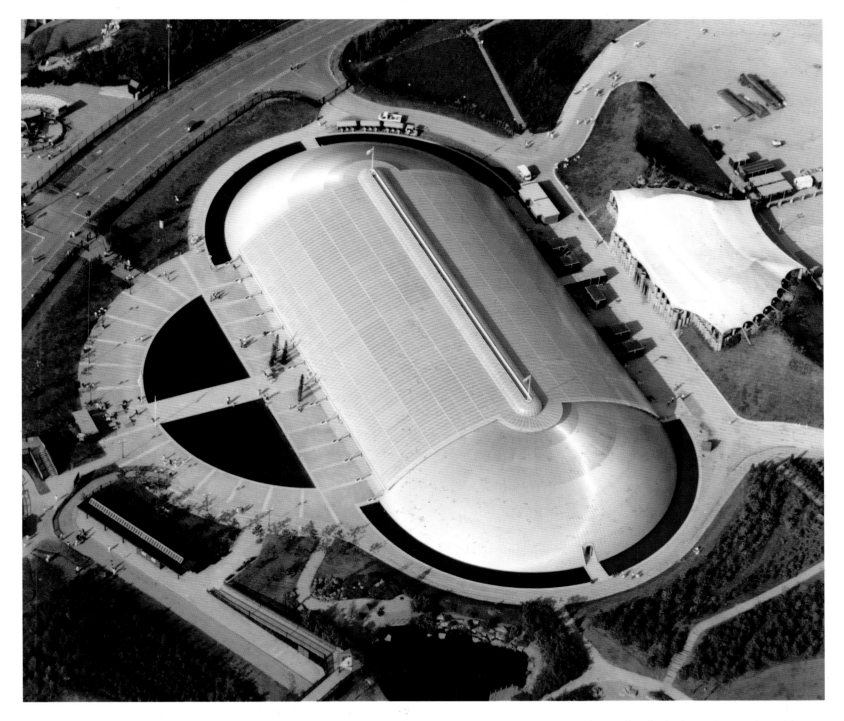

219 Pavilion for the International Garden Festival
     1984
     Sefton Street, Otterspool, L8
     Architects & Engineers: Arup Associates

A translucent structure, not unlike Lime Street Station, was built as the main architectural feature for the immensely successful International Garden Festival constructed on derelict land that had previously been used as a refuse dump. The gardens transformed that part of Liverpool and formed a fitting termination to the Otterspool Promenade. The building is a light and airy, pinned vault structure with a clear interior span. The graceful curved ends are roofed with aluminium sheeting specially formed, and the centre section with polycarbonate sheeting. Probably the finest new building to be built on Merseyside in the 1980s.

220 Tate Gallery of Liverpool

1988

Albert Dock, L1

Architect: Sir James Stirling, Michael Wilford & Associates

Jim Stirling, a master of museum architecture and a graduate of the Liverpool School of Architecture, did a splendid job in converting one side of the Albert Dock Warehouses into a modern art gallery without destroying either the feeling or the fabric of the old building. The result is both restrained in its handling of the structure and bold in its application of modern features. Strong lettering, vivid colour, blue and orange, and the use of the porthole symbol are all applied with panache and confidence to the new additions. The seven-storey block is converted into an entrance which rises in a double-height space with a mezzanine gallery along its back wall. Then three floors of galleries are ranged in the original warehouse spaces, the only interference to the visual impact of their iron structure and shallow-vaulted brick ceilings being the introduction of three long troughs suspended from the vaulting in each gallery, containing the lighting and ventilating services. The gallery has now been extended.

221 Liverpool School of Architecture & Building Engineering

1988

The University Precinct, Bedford Street North, Oxford Street, L3

Architects: Dave King & Rod McAllister in association with the Gerald Beech Partnership

When the Department of Building Engineering moved in with the School of Architecture it was clear that more accommodation was needed on the school site and so it was decided to rebuild the central courtyard which had once been open to the air, fitting in a new high-tech building. This has been admirably achieved to provide a lower exhibition hall and a large studio above, encircled by a gallery very much like a modern metal version of the traditional Non-conformist meeting hall. The detailing is beautifully consistent and the whole scheme is built on a series of composed shapes, something very difficult to carry out effectively in a conversion where the architects' hands are tied by the enclosing structure.

222 **Liverpool Sewage Treatment Works**
1989
Sandon Dock, Regent Road, L5
Architect: Athanassios Migos for Kingham Knight Associates

A large group of buildings and storage tanks built by North West Water as part of the Mersey Estuary Pollution Alleviation Scheme. It is something of a showpiece with its massive main block in blue and brindle engineering bricks rising austere and very much in character with the best traditional dock architecture. The central room, with its tiers of galleries and semi-circular concrete colonnade, is Classical in the grand scale, covered by a cruciform vault in polycarbonate. The pity is that the clients did not go one step further and accept the architects' suggestion to crown it with a dome in the tradition of the Mersey Docks and Harbour Board.

223 **Mahon Court**
1991
Upper Parliament Street, Parliament Place, L8
Architects: TACP

An exercise in 'keeping in keeping' and very acceptable in those terms for it has filled an ugly, bomb-torn gap and continues the rhythm of the Georgian terraces in Upper Parliament Street.

224 House in Grassendale Park

1991

29 South Road, Grassendale Park, L19

Architects: Irena Bauman & Maggie Pickles

A charming house designed with sympathy, taste and a sense of scale rare in modern domestic architecture, so that it sits comfortably in the sylvan setting of the park close to its Regency neighbours. The house was designed around a small courtyard that contained an ancient wisteria carefully protected during the construction stage. The result is magical. The design deservedly won the Daily Telegraph Homes Award.

225 Dean Walter's Building,
Liverpool John Moores University

1993

Anglican Cathedral Precinct, Rodney Street, L1

Architect: Keith Scott of Building Design Partnership

Standing by the approach to the west end of the Anglican Cathedral, this building, which contains the School of Media, Critical and Creative, is a lively attempt to 'keep in keeping' with the Georgian facades of Rodney Street and Mornington Terrace, but without adopting slavish imitation. There is a sort of Regency gaiety about its appearance with those tall, lightly-handled, curved windows flooding the interior with light.

226 **Aldham Robart's Learning Resource Centre, Liverpool John Moores University**
1994

Maryland Street, L1

Architects: Austin Smith Lord Engineers: Ove Arup & Partners

What, not long ago, we would have called a library, it now houses all the modern devices of communication and information, providing facilities for nearly seven thousand students and staff. It is a largely translucent cocoon of a building, every line controlled by sheated geometry. Hung in places on the outside there are asymmetrical panels of plain wall surface punched with a rhythm of square windows. Planes of glass,

ribs of metal and sheets of light play across its surfaces, particularly at night when it glows like a fairy palace. In plan, two main axes cross like the cardo and decumanus of a Roman castra, to create four quadrants on four floors, each marked by its glazed external staircase. But one quadrant has been hollowed out to form a three-storey entrance atrium set back and faced with a curved glass veneer. It is a lovely solution and the best piece of modern architecture in the city. It is hoped that the building, its main axis formed with that intention, will eventually be extended to join the back of now derelict St Andrew's Church [33], whose splendid Greek Revival portico will form a fitting ceremonial approach to the whole complex.

LIVERPOOL
city of architecture

Books & articles

This gazetteer is itself an introduction. It is hoped that it will whet the appetite for further investigation, and those who wish to pursue the subject are referred to the following books and articles:

CE Box *Liverpool Overhead Railway, 1893-1956*, revised edition, London 1962.

AT Brown *How Gothic came back to Liverpool*, Liverpool 1937.

Lionel B Budden *The Book of the Liverpool School of Architecture*, Liverpool & London 1932. This contains a short study of Charles Herbert Reilly, numerous drawings by students, including some by John Hughes, and buildings designed by graduates, many of which are on Merseyside.

Penelope Curtis *Sculpture on Merseyside*, Tate Gallery, Liverpool 1988.

Penelope Curtis, Editor *Patronage & Practice: Sculpture on Merseyside*, Tate Gallery, Liverpool 1989.

Department of the Environment *List of Buildings of Special Architectural and Historic Interest*, Liverpool 1975. The most valuable guide to the listed buildings of Liverpool.

Peter Fleetwood-Hesketh *Murray's Lancashire Architectural Guide*, London 1955. A very perceptive book written by a Liverpool architectural historian with a great respect for her buildings.

Quentin Hughes 'Dock Warehouses at Liverpool', *Architectural History*, Vol. IV, 1961.

Quentin Hughes *Seaport*, London 1964, new edition, Liverpool 1993.

Quentin Hughes 'Harvey Lonsdale Elmes and St George's Hall, Liverpool', *Architecture North West*, Vol. 24, August-September 1967. One of the first studies to illustrate Elmes' competition drawings for both the Assize Courts and the Hall.

Quentin Hughes *Liverpool*, London 1969. This is the book, published by Studio Vista, that has formed the basis of the present volume.

Quentin Hughes and Simon Pepper *Liverpool*, a typescript document issued for the visit of the Thirties Society to Liverpool in February 1982, Liverpool 1982.

Ronald P Jones 'The Life and Work of Harvey Lonsdale Elmes', *Architectural Review*, Vol. 15, No. 91, June 1904.

Peter Kennerley *The Building of Liverpool Cathedral*, Preston 1991.

Loraine Knowles *St George's Hall, Liverpool*, National Museums & Galleries on Merseyside, Liverpool 1988. A very useful study of the competition, the architects, the Great Hall, the Assize Courts, the Concert Room and the heating and ventilating.

Liverpool Heritage Bureau *Buildings of Liverpool*, Liverpool 1978.

Liverpool Heritage Bureau *Liverpool Conservation Areas*, Liverpool 1979, revised 1982.

Deidre Morley *Look Liverpool: Images of a Great Seaport*, with photographs by Alex Laing, Liverpool 1985.

Susan Nicholson, Editor *The Changing Face of Liverpool: 1207-1727*, Liverpool 1981.

Nikolaus Pevsner *The Buildings of England: South Lancashire*, Harmondsworth 1969. One of the series of indispensable volumes for any study of the buildings of England and Wales.

JA Picton *Architectural History of Liverpool*, Liverpool 1858.

JA Picton *Views in Modern Liverpool*, Liverpool 1864.

CH Reilly *Some Liverpool Streets and Buildings in 1921*, Liverpool 1921. A brilliant and very personal statement.

CH Reilly *Scaffolding in the Sky*, London 1938.

Thomas Rickman *An Attempt to Discriminate the Styles of English Architecture from the Conquest to the Reformation; Preceded by a Sketch of the Grecian and Roman Orders*, London 1817. This was printed by J & J Smith in Liverpool.

Thomas Miller Rickman *Notes on the Life and on the Several Imprints of the Work of Thomas Rickman, FSA, Architect, collected by his son*, London 1901.

Nancy Ritchie-Noakes *Jesse Hartley: Dock Engineer to the Port of Liverpool 1824-60*, Liverpool 1980.

Nancy Ritchie-Noakes *Liverpool's Historic Waterfront*, HMSO, London 1984.

Joseph Sharples *The Oratory: St James's Cemetery Liverpool*, National Museums and Galleries on Merseyside, Liverpool 1991.

FM Simpson 'Liverpool Cathedral – its site and style', *Architectural Review*, Vol. 10, 1901.

Colin Wilkinson & Michael Meadows *Liverpool Then and Now*, Liverpool 1991.

John Willett *Art in a City*, London 1967. Although this is primarily a masterly study of Liverpool painters and sculptors, it contains many references to architecture and opening chapters on 'Problems and Place' and 'Views of the Past' which are relevant.